To Live as Francis Lived

To Live as Francis Lived
A GUIDE FOR SECULAR FRANCISCANS

LEONARD FOLEY, O.F.M.

JOVIAN WEIGEL, O.F.M.

PATTI NORMILE, S.F.O.

ST. ANTHONY MESSENGER PRESS
Cincinnati, Ohio

Nihil Obstat: Rev. Nicholas Lohkamp, O.F.M.
           Rev. Robert J. Hagedorn

Imprimi Potest: Rev. Fred Link, O.F.M.

Imprimatur: +Most Rev. Carl K. Moeddel, V.G.
           Archdiocese of Cincinnati
           February 17, 2000

The *nihil obstat* and *imprimatur* are a declaration that a book is considered to be free from doctrinal or moral error. It is not implied that those who have granted the *nihil obstat* and *imprimatur* agree with the contents, opinions or statements expressed.

Cover photo by Gene Plaisted, O.S.C., of a painting
in St. Stephen Episcopal Church, Orinda, CA
Cover and book design by Constance Wolfer

ISBN 0-86716-396-8

Dedication

To Live as Francis Lived is dedicated to
Father Leonard Foley, O.F.M., and
Father Jovian Weigel, O.F.M.,
Franciscans who have blessed the
Secular Franciscan Order and its members
with much love, support and
spiritual wisdom.

The Secular Franciscan Order

"The Lord give you peace!"

Dear Reader:

You have in your hands a book that has been requested by many who try to live life today in the spirit in which Francis of Assisi lived eight centuries ago. The heart of this book is the message of *The Third Order Vocation*, a book that caught the hearts of Franciscans and those who long to follow Francis.

Our goal is to retain the simplicity and the spirit of Franciscan living expressed by Franciscan Fathers Leonard Foley and Jovian Weigel in *The Third Order Vocation* book while adding new material to harmonize the work with The Rule of the Secular Franciscan Order approved by Pope Paul VI in 1978 and the revised General Constitutions of the Secular Franciscan Order. We hope this book will speak to you about a deeper way of Christian living through the let's-sit-down-and-talk-about-it writing style of Father Leonard coupled with the vital Franciscan spirituality of Father Jovian.

The primary focus of *To Live As Francis Lived* is to form believers in the Franciscan way of life either as professed members of the Secular Franciscan Order or as friends of Francis and Clare. That can be accomplished only through prayer, reflection and action. This book is first, therefore, a *prayer book*. No deep understanding of Jesus, Francis and Clare can be reached without God's direction through prayer. As you study the text and suggested additional readings, as you read Articles from the Rule of the Secular Franciscan Order which appear in various chapters, meditate on Questions for Reflection, consider the Application to Daily Life and concluding prayers. Make each action part of your prayer life.

Invite the Holy Spirit to lead you not just to "head knowledge" of Francis and Clare but to a deep spiritual understanding that will result in your conversion. Conversion is the ongoing process of learning to live the gospel way of life given to us by Jesus and revealed to us by Francis and Clare.

No single publication can serve as the sole text for understanding

Francis and Clare of Assisi. At the conclusion of this book you will find an extensive list of writings by and about Francis and Clare. Readings from those books may be suggested in this work. *To Live as Francis Lived* is intended to lead you into a new relationship with Jesus Christ in the manner of Francis and Clare. That applies whether you are a professed Franciscan of many years or one just beginning to seek a spiritual understanding of these most beloved saints.

We invite you to enter into a process of study, prayer and action to learn more about living the Christian life in the twenty-first century in the way Francis lived it in his time.

Leonard Foley, O.F.M.

Jovian Weigel, O.F.M.

Patti Normile, S.F.O.

*L*ord, make me an instrument of your peace,
where there is hatred, let me sow love;
where there is injury, pardon;
where there is doubt, faith;
where there is despair, hope;
where there is darkness, light;
and where there is sadness, joy.

O Divine Master, grant that I may not
so much seek to be consoled
   as to console,
to be understood, as to understand,
to be loved as to love.

For it is in giving that we receive,
it is in pardoning that we are pardoned,
and it is in dying
that we are born to eternal life.

—*Attributed to Saint Francis of Assisi*

Exhortation of Saint Francis

Dearly beloved brothers and eternally blessed children, hear me, hear the voice of your Father. We have promised great things, greater things have been promised to us. Let us keep the former, and long for the latter. Pleasure is brief, punishment eternal. Suffering is slight, glory infinite. Many are called, few chosen. To all an award will be made.

Contents

The Apostolates

Structure

Introduction

Welcome to the family of Saint Francis. A most beautiful quality of Francis was his courtesy. He welcomed all who came to him. And so we welcome you in your quest to discover the spirit of Saint Francis.

Some of you are entering a new experience of discovering the Franciscan way of life. Jesus promises "a new heaven and a new earth." He came to establish his Father's kingdom. That newness and that task are your calling. You are entering into an exciting new world. You may choose to become a member of a new family—the Franciscan family. As you read, study, pray, you will become more and more conscious of yourself as a child of God and a brother or sister of Jesus. You can expect the Holy Spirit to work in you in a new way, together with your brothers and sisters in faith.

> [T]hose who wait for the LORD shall renew their strength,
> they shall mount up with wings like eagles
> they shall run and not be weary, they shall walk and not faint.
> (Isaiah 40:31)

You may have doubts about what all of this means. But as Jesus calls you, he also says: "Do not fear. I am with you."

A Franciscan Creed

The Secular Franciscan Order (formerly known as the Third Order of Saint Francis) is in its eighth century of existence. Through these centuries, the Lord has gathered people together in the way of Francis. The shared vision of Francis and his followers has sustained and nourished millions of people along this way. Their vision is contained in the following Creed based on the guidelines set by the 1969 Assisi Third Order Congress:

> Inspired by the vision of Saint Francis, we commit ourselves to the Gospel as our way of life.
>
> Our world-view is centered in Christ; we see Jesus Christ as the beginning, the way and the goal of all creation.
>
> This world vision reveals to us a God who is Father and a life which is love. This demands of us a life as brothers and sisters of all

people and of creation.

    We are on pilgrimage, trying to reach our Father, trying to live a life of love. We have not yet arrived; we are sinners, but we are called to be saints.

    As sinners, weak human beings, we must undergo a continuing conversion, returning always to the Father as prodigal sons and daughters.

    Christ was poor and Christ was crucified; we seek to share in his poorness and in his suffering. We further commit ourselves to the service of the poor.

    In making our way through life, we are guided more by simplicity, humility and littleness rather than by power, prestige and status.

    Like Christ, like Francis, we seek to become instruments of peace, peacemakers.

    Acknowledging the guiding presence of the Holy Spirit, we declare our loyalty to the Church in a spirit of dialogue and cooperation with her ministers and shepherds.

    We are conscious of our obligation to share in the life and mission of the Church. We are lay apostles called by Christ to continue his work on earth.

    Our life and our spirituality, however, is characteristically secular, in the world and for the world.

    Joy sustains our lives, fulfills our living; we seek the same for others.

    To achieve all this is difficult; hence we declare our need for Christ's Eucharist, for personal, communal and liturgical prayer.

Suggestions on How to Use This Book

This book is divided into reflections that can be used to span a year by contemplating one aspect of the Franciscan way each week. Through these reflections you will learn about the Franciscan way of life. There is no need to rush through the reflections. Take as many days or weeks as you need with each reflection to discover what the Lord is saying to you.

    If you choose a weekly approach, each week you are invited to study the material presented, reflect on it and pray over it. The way to Jesus through Francis and Clare of Assisi is not the same for any two people. Therefore, it is not necessary to begin with Reflection 1 and proceed through Reflection 52. You may have a need to reflect on a particular topic. Look for that topic in the Table of Contents and spend time with it. We hope you will reflect on all the chapters at some time.

    After reading and reflecting on the topic, consider the questions at the end of the lesson under the title: "Questions for Reflection." This is not an examination but an opportunity for you to express yourself—where you are going, where you are growing. It may be helpful to write your thoughts as you grow in Francis's way of following the Lord.

You may wish to share your answers and thoughts with someone accompanying you on your spiritual journey. That person may be a spiritual director, a spiritual friend or the formation director of a Secular Franciscan fraternity. Sharing may clarify your understanding. We want you to be thoroughly familiar with the Franciscan way of life which you are considering entering as a professed member or as a friend of Francis and Clare.

In each lesson you will find "Connecting with Scripture" in which we suggest a Scripture reading. These readings do not have a particular connection with the reflection they follow. But if you are serious about "living the Gospel," you will need to know what Jesus said and did and these Scriptures will provide that.

Francis received his guidance from the Spirit by taking the Word of God very seriously, reading it regularly. We must do the same so that it may "make a home" in us.

The questions under the title "Application to Daily Life" are for your own private reflection. Answer them faithfully, prayerfully and honestly to see how Francis is affecting your life. The activity suggested in "Application to Daily Life" is essential because the way of Francis is not so much a way of thinking as a way of living. We should feel a sense of urgency in following the way of the Lord, yet at the same time remain people of peace and hope.

Each reflection concludes with a brief prayer related to the topic reflected upon. That prayer is designed to continue your own conversation or listening time with the Lord.

We suggest that you begin a journal. This journal is for no one but yourself. Write down insights the Holy Spirit sends you, prayers and thoughts that enlighten you. You will find that you progress a great deal, even though the growth may seem almost imperceptible at the time.

Finally, we suggest that you read *Francis: The Journey and the Dream*, by Father Murray Bodo, O.F.M. Each week, we suggest reading a certain number of pages. You will learn that the Franciscan life is an experience of spiritual life rather than a collection of useful information. Father Murray describes the book in this way:

> This book is my own Dream and my own Journey with Francis. My prayer is that the Dream will come clear for you, that you will be challenged, too, to set out on a journey with Francis to that Peace and Joy that surpasses all understanding.

Other readings are suggested from *The Way of St. Francis* and *Clare: A Light in the Garden* by Father Bodo, and *Following Francis of Assisi:*

A Spirituality for Daily Living by Patti Normile, S.F.O.

Have a Plan for Study

You will need some kind of work plan to discipline yourself and to keep you from drifting aimlessly. We suggest that you:

- Set aside a definite time for study each week. Sunday afternoon? Wednesday night? Every afternoon at four?
- Make this a definite length of time. Ten minutes? Half an hour? An hour?
- Write down "My Plan For Study and Reading." Day of week____ Time of day____ How long?____

Set a Time for Prayer

Certainly you can pray anytime and anywhere, but some planning is most important. Growing in the way of Francis will lead you to know Jesus intimately, so you will feel the need to speak with him. Ask yourself, "At what time or times of the day can I best pray?" "How much time can I give to prayer?" Set aside a definite time for prayer. Pray any way you wish: in your own words, using a prayer book, using Scripture, the Rosary, some form of "The Liturgy of the Hours." But have a plan! We suggest you write down "My Plan for Praying:" Time of day____ How long?____

For the Professed

These reflections can also benefit committed professed Secular Franciscans. We forget sometimes! And we always need to continue to study and to pray if we expect to grow in the way of the Lord. Allow the Holy Spirit to revive your own Franciscan Spirit through these reflections.

A Special Note

The Rule of the Secular Franciscan Order that is presented in sidebars throughout *To Live As Francis Lived* is a valuable tool for prayer and reflection. The Articles of the Rule are not presented in numerical order but appear where they relate to a particular topic. However, the entire Rule together with the Letter to All the Faithful written by Saint Francis himself, is included in an appendix at the end of the book. This Rule was approved by Pope Paul VI in 1978 as the guide for people living in the secular world who wish to follow Francis of Assisi. Secular Franciscans are not *ordained* Franciscans, though ordained diocesan priests and deacons are invited to explore membership in the S.F.O. Youth groups are affiliated with some Secular Franciscan fraternities.

If you have not already done so, should you wish to live this life, you are invited to join in formation with a Secular Franciscan Fraternity. Secular Franciscan fraternities and youth groups can be located by consulting with Franciscans in your area or by calling 1-800-FRANCIS for information.

A Final Note

We are responding to your desire for a closer life with the Lord, to your search for God. On this journey, look for someone to help you along, to discuss confusing things with you, to help you over the rough spots. This might be the Spiritual Assistant in your Secular Franciscan fraternity or a person with whom you can share your relationship with the Lord. All of us need help along the way.

God bless you on your way to him!

The Foundation

he foundation of the Franciscan way of life is Jesus Christ and no other. To follow Francis's way is to strive with all our bodies, minds and spirits to go from "gospel to life and life to the gospel." To begin to accomplish that, we must know the gospel of Jesus in order to live our lives in accord with it. To know the gospel we must know the Lord. That is the direction toward which each of the following reflections lead us. We who have followed Jesus now begin again to bring our lives into the gospel life, the gospel into our everyday lives.

REFLECTION 1

Beginning Again

"Let us begin to do good, for as yet we have done little."
—Saint Francis

Saint Francis spoke these words at a time when most people already considered him a saint. In his mind, there was no plateau in life where he could feel he had "made it" and could coast into heaven from then on. He did not compare his love with that of other men but with that of Christ; hence he always saw an infinite expanse into which he could still go, becoming more and more like his Lord.

So it is with you, whether you are a professed Secular Franciscan, a candidate wishing to become a Secular Franciscan or one interested in learning more about Francis's way of following Jesus. God has already blessed you with his life and given you the gift of faith and faithfulness possibly through many years of life. But, because you have chosen to read *To Live as Francis Lived*, you are one who wants to begin again as Francis always did.

Each time we begin anew, we enter a new phase of life intent on enriching our relationship with God through the inspiration of Saint Francis and Saint Clare together with their brothers and sisters. You are not entering upon something *different* from the Christian life or something better than the life of other Christians. You are looking, like Francis and with Francis, into that vast expanse of Christ's love and desiring to share it more deeply. *The only thing "different" about your new life is that your Christian life will now be given a particular coloring and direction by Saint Francis and the traditions that have grown from his life and words.* You're beginning again, and you will continue to begin again for the rest of your life. Congratulations!

New Beginnings

For those wishing to pursue professed membership in the Secular Franciscan Order, you need to be linked with a fraternity in your area. The journey to profession begins with a period of inquiry into the meaning of Franciscan fraternity life. Interested individuals are then invited to become candidates. A minimum of one year's formation done with the formation director or team of a fraternity follows. You are already committed to Christ. Now you will let him deepen that commitment by following the Rule of the Secular Franciscan Order. The formation period involves solid grounding, both theoretical and practical, in the Christian life as seen through the eyes of Saint Francis. While profession in the Secular Franciscan Order requires membership in the Catholic Church, the S.F.O. maintains a friendly relationship with followers of Francis who belong to other Christian churches. In this book we will call these faithful ones friends of Francis. Information on these groups is also available by calling 1-800-FRANCIS.

Commitment and Formation

Never forget, as long as you live, that the final purpose of the Secular Franciscan Order must be to help you fulfill the great commandment: "[Y]ou shall love the Lord your God with all your heart, and with all your soul, and with all your mind, and with all your strength.... 'You shall love your neighbor as yourself'" (Mark 12:30-31). Your purpose as a Secular Franciscan or a friend of Francis is to fulfill the purpose God gave you: to respond to his love with total love of your own—to commit yourself, to consecrate yourself, to dedicate yourself completely to the good God.

"Formation" is more than instruction. You will ask God to bring a new "form" or style into your life—through the influence and inspiration of Saint Francis. God's response will be your tranSFOrmation into the individual you are created to be. It takes a lifetime but it is more than worth the effort.

Conditions for admission to the Secular Franciscan Order are: "...to profess the Catholic faith, to live in communion with the Church, to be of good moral standing, and to show clear signs of a vocation" (General Constitutions, Article 39, 2).

Can Anybody Be "Perfect"?

Pope Pius XII said, "Although the Third Order (the former name of the Secular Franciscan Order) is not a body of people who are already perfect, it is above all a school of Christian perfection imbued with the genuine Franciscan spirit. For it was instituted for this purpose: to satisfy fully the sincere desires of those who had to remain in the world but who do not wish to be of the world. The S.F.O. (Third Order) directs its appeal to those who burn with the desire of striving for perfection in their own station in life" (Address to Tertiaries, 1956).

Don't take that word "perfection" in the wrong way. It's not something you do. It's not like those "thermometers" put up on the courthouse lawn to indicate how close we are to the $300,000 needed for new fire trucks. You can't, and you shouldn't, ever try to "measure" your perfection, still less compare your rank and rating with anyone else's. "Perfection" simply means being like God. It's not an obligation; it's a gift. It's not something you do; it's what God does. It's the whole purpose of God's eternal plan—to make us like God. So God says, "Be perfect. Be like me. Love as I do. But you can't do it by yourself. My Spirit in you will be your power."

The "School" Has a Textbook

The "school" Pope Pius spoke of is the community of men and women who are moved by the shared vision of Francis. The textbook of that school is the Gospel, the inspired faith-vision written down by the Church in the New Testament. This is primary. Any additions such as the Rule and Constitution are merely attempts to make some practical suggestions about carrying out the gospel in the circumstances of the twenty-first century. And while the Gospel is the textbook, the Holy Spirit is the instructor.

A School Has Many Grades

A tree grows gradually, a thousandth of an inch a day. In your spiritual life, you must be satisfied to progress only gradually, like the tree. Usually you will not notice your growth. Sometimes it may even seem you are growing backward as you discover your weaknesses and failings. But trust in God. Allow God to lead you—through your formation director, through your spiritual companion, through the reflections of this book, through your own study and prayer.

Week by week, you will turn your attention from one aspect of the spiritual life to another. It's like painting a picture: a touch here, a dab there, and gradually the masterpiece emerges. There is just one difference. When you finish this year of reflection, study and prayer, you will be just beginning a deeper and more fruitful life with God.

Fraternity Meetings

For those of you who are professed or aspiring to profession, attendance at fraternity gatherings is essential. In fraternity is where the Secular Franciscan Order is best experienced as a family. Coming together will be a source of living instruction and inspiration.

Your Obligation

It may sound legalistic to say so, but let it be said anyway: In becoming a member of the Secular Franciscan Order, you do not incur any obligations that bind you under pain of sin. It is presumed, of course, that you are serious about the ideals and practices of the Secular Franciscan Order and that you will not ask to make profession unless you have a sincere intention to live the Franciscan way throughout your life.

Beginning Again

Your immediate goal for this year is profession in the S.F.O.—or perhaps just a renewed, Franciscan commitment to Jesus. You are welcome to attend fraternity gatherings as an inquirer. If you wish to become a candidate and are approved by your Franciscan brothers and sisters, you will promise to "live more intensely and faithfully the grace and dedication of...Baptism by following Jesus Christ according to the teachings and example of St. Francis of Assisi" (*Ritual*, p. 14). The purpose of your time as an inquirer and a candidate is to help you and prepare you in making this decision. And when you have made profession, you will begin again (General Constitutions, Articles 37-43).

Questions for Reflection—In what ways do you hope to deepen your love of God? What mistakes have you made in the past that have kept you from God? What attitude in you has been the greatest hindrance to deepening your love of God? Do you feel you can have a better spirit formed in you?

Connecting With Scripture and Franciscan Writings—Christ's birth and early life in Luke, Chapters 1-2, and Matthew, Chapter 1:18-25. Bodo, *Francis: The Journey and the Dream*, pp. v-5.

Application to Daily Life—Experiment this week with the best time—and length of time—to reflect, study and pray each day. Make your plan realistic—don't try too much.

Prayer—Lord, you promise to make all things new. That includes me. As I begin this journey to discover Saint Francis's way to you, I ask you to begin to renew my faith, my hope and my love. Amen.

REFLECTION 2

The Nature and Purpose of the Secular Franciscan Order

"The Third (Secular Franciscan) Order is equally for clerics and lay-folk, maidens, widows and married people. The intention of the Brothers and Sisters of Penance is to live honorably in their residences and to busy themselves with pious actions and to flee from the vanities of the world."

—Bernard of Bessa, Secretary of Saint Bonaventure

The Franciscan Movement

Francis, as you know or will learn from reading about his life, simply wanted to follow the gospel literally, wholeheartedly and humbly. Others were inspired by his example and captured by his vision. In a comparatively short time the little group of Franciscans grew into an order of thousands which needed organization. Francis was careful to have every development of the Order approved by the Holy Father. The original Rule, a collection of Gospel texts, became the final and definitive Rule of 1223 which First Order Franciscans still observe today.

Over nearly eight centuries, the Order has had its ups and downs. There have been periods of great spiritual fervor, and also times when the vision of Francis was somewhat eclipsed. Today there are three branches of what is called the "First" Order of Saint Francis: the Friars Minor (O.F.M.), the Capuchins (O.F.M. Cap.) and the Conventuals (O.F.M. Conv.). When Saint Clare and other women followed the example of Francis, the "Second Order" was founded, known today as the Poor Clares.

Some members of the "Third" Order of Saint Francis band together to live in community, take the three vows of poverty, chastity and obedience, and observe a rule approved by the Holy See. They are therefore called Third Order "Regulars" (T.O.R.) and comprise most of the Franciscan sisters with whom you may be familiar. You may be preparing to enter the Secular Franciscan Order formerly known as the Third Order Secular, that is, Franciscans who live in the world as lay men and women.

How the Third Order Started

On one of his wanderings Francis met a merchant named Luchesio in the town of Poggibonsi. Luchesio had been a rather hard man who watched his money very carefully, though he was strangely generous to the poor, gave lodging to pilgrims and helped widows and orphans. Francis seems to have had no influence in his conversion but gave him and his wife, Bona Donna, a norm of life. After this Luchesio devoted all his time to works of charity, especially care of the sick in the hospitals. He wore a rough tunic of a simple peasant with a rope around his waist. When he was home, he worked in a little garden he had retained after parting with his other possessions and whose produce he sold. If this way of life did not bring him enough, he would go out and beg.

A number of people with the same spirit gathered around Luchesio. Francis gave these followers (later called the Brothers and Sisters of Penance which means those who turn to God from a sinful and idle life) a rule of life. They sought to imitate *in the world* the ways of Saint Francis and his Brothers. As soon as they entered the Brotherhood, they pledged themselves to give back all unjustly acquired goods—which in many cases meant to give up everything—to pay the tithes which they might owe, to make their wills in time to prevent strife among their heirs, not to bear arms, not to take an oath except in special extraordinary cases, and not to accept public office. They wore a poor and distinctive habit and divided their time between prayer and deeds of charity. They generally lived with their families, but sometimes, like the Friars Minor, they withdrew into solitude.

They soon came into conflict with the public authorities because of their principles. At Faenza, for instance, the citizens had joined the Brotherhood in great numbers. The mayor wanted them to take the usual oath of obedience by which they would oblige themselves to take up arms when the authorities ordered it. They refused; taking up arms was against their Rule. The dispute soon spread all over Italy. As a sort of punishment the cities subjected the Penitential Brothers to special taxes and forbade them to give their property to the poor. Cardinal Hugolino, friend of Saint Francis, took up their defense. When he became Pope, he ordered the clergy to take the side of the Penitential Brothers and to see that they were not injured in any way.

The Pope wished to unite the scattered brotherhoods into one body. Around 1221, Cardinal Hugolino and Francis wrote the first formal Rule for the Third Order. We do not have this rule, but it was certainly the foundation of the Rule of 1228 which we do have.

Holiness in the World

For nearly eight centuries, this gathering of the faithful has been striving to live the Gospel life *in the world* under the direction of the Franciscan Order and according to the Rule of Saint Francis as approved and adapted by the Church.

It is therefore: a) a brother/sisterhood of lay people (though diocesan clergy may also be members), b) attempting to live the evangelical life "in the world," in the ordinary circumstances of the life of lay people, in home and school, factory and office, c) following a Rule or way of life, d) with spiritual assistance from other branches of the Franciscan family or certified individuals, e) approved and adapted by the Church. Whatever else Francis was, he was Catholic, seriously concerned to have the approval of the Church at a time when many reformers, in good or bad faith, were attempting to reform the Church by tearing down its structure or leaving it altogether.

A True Order

The Secular Franciscan Order is distinguished from other lay associations in the Church in that its primary purpose is the striving to live the gospel life. Other groups may have a specific purpose. For example, the Confraternity of Christian Doctrine was formed for the special purpose of fostering religious instruction. As a lay order, the Secular Franciscan Order stresses fraternity life, a quest for personal holiness and personal and fraternity apostolates as way of living for social justice and peace among all people.

Questions for Reflection—What is the primary purpose of the Secular Franciscan Order? What other purposes does the S.F.O. fulfill?

Connecting With Scripture and Franciscan Writings—Beginning of Christ's public life in Luke, Chapters 3-4 and in John, Chapter 1:19-51 and Chapter 2. Bodo, pp. 6-8.

Application to Daily Life—Does belonging to an order of lay people call for changes in your life? What discipline of life is involved in becoming a Secular Franciscan? Pray each day that the way of Saint Francis may affect your whole life, that you may truly be a holy person living in the world.

Prayer—Thank you, Lord, for the faithful ones who have followed you in the way of Saint Francis through the centuries. Open my heart and mind to discern if the Franciscan way of life is my call to spiritual life. Amen.

From the Rule of the Secular Franciscan Order

1. The Franciscan family, as one among many spiritual families raised up by the Holy Spirit in the Church, unites all members of the People of God—laity, religious, and priests—who recognize that they are called to follow Christ in the footsteps of Saint Francis of Assisi.

   In various ways and forms but in life-giving union with each other, they intend to make present the charism of their common Seraphic Father in the life and mission of the Church.

REFLECTION 3

The Mission of the Secular Franciscan Order Is to Live the Gospel Life

"[A]fter the Lord gave me some brothers, no one showed me what I had to do, but the Most High Himself revealed to me that I should live according to the pattern of the Holy Gospel. And I had this written down simply and in a few words and the Lord Pope confirmed it for me."

—*Saint Francis*, The Testament

The Foundation of Francis's Life

It is impossible to capture Saint Francis in an analysis or a summary. Where grace is, there is mystery. But if, in a human way, we try to list the elements of the mystery, we would have to place the Gospel at the head of that list. In his delightful and even thrilling literalness, Francis simply said, "Here is God's living Word. He is speaking to us today. What other 'rule' do we need?"

What Francis meant by "Gospel" was *Jesus*, the living Word of God made living flesh and living with us today. "Brothers, I know Holy Writ—I know the poor Christ," he said. The last thing Francis wanted was to be "special" or to found a group of people who would be distinguished or superior. He simply wanted as many people as possible to be led by the Holy Spirit to live the Gospel of Jesus Christ, allowing the Lord to transform their lives. To be a Franciscan, then, is to attempt to be Christian, a disciple. As we have said, something distinctive *did* happen: Saint Francis. So Franciscans today are "distinct" (though Saint Francis wouldn't like the word!) by trying to be Christians with the particular inspiration and tradition of Saint Francis. Nevertheless, the fundamental thrust is always the gospel way of life. A way of life is a set of values, a spirit that affects our whole life, an attitude that enters into every thought we think, each emotion we feel, what we say and each action of our days. Christianity is the way of life God himself has graciously given us. Our tradition says: "Since Christ is the way, the truth, and the life, Secular Franciscans should have the deep conviction that, by Baptism and profession they must become like Christ crucified, and follow his Gospel as their rule of life. As they live their lives in the world, they are imbued with the mind and spirit of Christ."

The Gospel Is the Good News

We can never emphasize enough the fact that "Gospel" means "Good News." This is one of the key ideas in Saint Francis's life. He was thrilled to discover the beauty and simplicity of this idea: The Good News is that God is our Father and our Mother! God loves us! Christ is our Brother. We are the children of God, truly possessing spiritual life. We are brothers and sisters of Christ and of each other. The Spirit of God's love lives in us. Our lives are holy and secure in Christ. Christ and his Gospel were, therefore, the center of the life of Saint Francis. They must be the center of Secular Franciscan life. We are to live the gospel—that is, live according to the Good News! Live as God's children, brothers and sisters of Christ, temples of the Holy Spirit. Practically every detail of life has been "modeled" for us on the earthly life of Christ.

Let's Get Specific

1) *The Bible*—Since the Word of God was vital to Francis, reading and praying with Scripture is a fundamental practice of our life. More will be said on this in another chapter.

2) *The Rule*—Francis's first Rule, approved verbally in 1209, was made up for the most part from passages from Holy Scripture. In 1221, Pope Honorius III placed the Brothers and Sisters of Penance near Rimimi, Italy, under the protection of the bishop. The same year, Pope Honorius III approved the Third Order. Pope Nicholas IV issued a uniform Rule in 1289. This Rule was followed until 1883 when Pope Leo III adapted it to modern conditions while retaining its essential spirit. In 1957, the Sacred Congregation of Religious issued General Constitutions for the Third Order. Today, Secular Franciscans from all over the world follow the Rule approved and confirmed by Pope Paul VI on June 24, 1978.

The Rule is not a list of do's and do not's. (Some part of it must necessarily be strictly "legal"—for instance, directions about organizations and procedures.) But the Rule is primarily a positive guide to Christian living. The Church says, as it were: "Your...Rule and the Constitutions present the gospel life for you. If you make a generous effort to follow them, you will be living the gospel life."

3) *The Spirit of the Rule*—Key points of the gospel which Francis emphasized will also be emphasized in this book: a spirit of intimacy with the Lord, a spirit of brotherly/sisterly love, a spirit of service towards all, a spirit of simplicity and constant change of heart.

A Generous Spirit

Franciscan life is a high calling. But if God has given us this vocation, he will also give us his grace to carry it out. One important quality is required: a spirit of trust and generosity. This is the lesson of Saint Francis's life: a spirit of childlike confidence in his Father in heaven, and in the power and wisdom and love of his Father. With him, there is nothing to fear. Nothing can hurt us. There is no problem we cannot solve with God's wisdom and grace.

Questions for Reflection—What is a way of life? What does the Secular Franciscan Order add to the Christian way of life? What is the Good News? How are we told how to live the gospel life?

Connecting With Scripture and Franciscan Writings—Christ's early ministry in John, Chapters 3-4; Luke, Chapters 5-6. Bodo, pp. 8-10. Normile, *Following Francis of Assisi*, Chapter 5.

Application to Daily Life—Do you think of your life as an observance of the gospel? Why was Saint Francis so concerned about the "Gospel" life? Do you share the "Good News" with others? If the gospel is the "Good News," should religion be glad or sad? As you read the Gospel, the Rule and the Constitutions, try to think of practical ways to apply the Gospel to your daily life at home, in the workplace, among friends.

Prayer—I praise you, Lord, for the Good News, your Gospel of truth which can lead me to life's great truth. Keep me faithful to your teachings. Amen.

From the Rule of the Secular Franciscan Order

2. The Secular Franciscan Order holds a special place in this family circle. It is an organic union of all Catholic fraternities scattered throughout the world and open to every group of the faithful. In these fraternities the brothers and sisters, led by the Spirit, strive for perfect charity in their own secular state. By their profession they pledge themselves to live the gospel in the manner of Saint Francis by means of this rule approved by the Church.

REFLECTION 4

Franciscan Spirituality

Most High, all-powerful, good Lord,
    Yours are the praises, the glory, *and* the honor, *and*
      all blessing,
To You alone, Most High, do they belong,
    and no human is worthy to mention Your name.
. . .
Praise *and* bless *my* Lord *and give Him thanks*
    and serve Him with great humility.

—*Saint Francis*, The Testament

What Is a "Spirituality"?

A spirituality is a particular *way,* or *emphasis,* in following Christ. Obviously many things are common to all Christians, and these are more important than the interests of any one group of Christians: Christlike love and forgiveness, community, personal and communal prayer, celebration of the sacramental life of the Church, obedience to legitimate authority, love of Scripture and concern for justice and peace, to name a few. There is no difference in our goals and in many of our ways and means. But there can be a difference in what can only be called *emphasis.* We speak of a Benedictine, a Dominican, a Franciscan spirituality. There is a spirituality proper to lay people, as contrasted with that of priests or that of nuns and brothers.

Perhaps the idea can best be illustrated in this way. Several bands may each play the same piece. But the results from a rock group playing are not the same as those heard on your public broadcasting station! Or a variety of vocalists may sing the "Star Spangled Banner" at ball games around the country with sounds so varied you may wonder if it is the same national anthem. Or several writers may describe the same events or persons; but if one reads accounts of the American Revolution written from a British or an American viewpoint the tone would be quite different!

The Way of Francis

Differing spiritualities depend largely on the personalities of their founders and the times in which religious communities developed. Pope Pius XII described it this way: "The spirituality of any saint is his particular way of picturing God to himself, of speaking to him, of approaching him. Every saint sees the attributes of God in the light of what he ponders most, of what penetrates him most deeply, of what attracts and conquers him. For every saint, one particular virtue of Christ is the ideal toward which he must tend. Yet all the saints— indeed the whole Church—strive to imitate the whole Christ."

Saint Francis, "Special"?

One Franciscan writer has said, "If anything specific can be observed about Saint Francis, it is his great concern to desire *nothing* specific." Francis's spirituality was simply to "observe the Gospel." Yet because he was a unique and attractive personality, the Church gained a unique charism called Franciscan spirituality. Pius XII further stated: "There is, then, a Franciscan doctrine in accordance with which God is holy, is great, and above all, is good, indeed the supreme Good. For in this doctrine, *God is love.* He lives by love, creates for love, becomes flesh and redeems, that is, he saves and makes holy, for love. There is also a Franciscan way of contemplating Jesus...in his human love." The great Franciscan emphasis, then, is on the fact that God is love. Every Christian believes this, of course. Franciscans choose to emphasize it as Saint Francis did.

Are Franciscans "Superior"?

If Saint Francis could blush in heaven, he would be embarrassed at any hint that his Order, or his Way, or his spirituality set him or his friends "above" anyone else. In fact, one of the essential elements of his spirituality was being "lesser" and having his followers be "lesser" brothers and sisters.

One spirituality is not superior to another; it is merely different. I am moved by Calvary, you are touched by Bethlehem. Some feel that judgment and watchfulness should be our greatest concern; others emphasize the patience and mercy of God. None of us is better; we are what we are. There is something that makes a Spaniard different from an Irishman—not better, just distinct.

Elements of Franciscan Spirituality

This book is an attempt to express both the overall Christian spirituality as well as a Franciscan one. As a summary, we list these elements.

To live the gospel according to the spirit of Saint Francis:

- in communion with Christ poor and crucified,
- in the love of God,
- in brother/sisterhood with all people and all of creation,
- participating in the life and mission of the Church,
- in continual conversion,
- in a life of prayer—liturgical, personal, communal,
- as instruments of peace.

Questions for Reflection—What is the difference between various spiritualities? What is your image of God? What is unique about Franciscan spirituality? Why does Franciscan spirituality attract you?

Connecting With Scripture and Franciscan Writings—The Sermon on the Mount in Matthew, Chapters 5-7. Bodo, pp. 10-12; Normile, *Following Francis of Assisi*, Chapter 1.

Application to Daily Life—What application does "God is Love" have on your worries, your prayer, your work, your family life, your relationships with others? Does the fact that you are attracted to the Franciscan way indicate anything special about your personality? This week try to recall, as often as you can, the fact that "God is Love."

Prayer—Lord, I invite your Spirit to guide me into your way, into your love. I will try to follow you all the days of my life. Amen.

From the Rule of the Secular Franciscan Order

4. The rule and life of the Secular Franciscans is this: to observe the gospel of our Lord Jesus Christ by following the example of Saint Francis of Assisi, who made Christ the inspiration and the center of his life with God and people.

   Christ, the gift of the Father's love, is the way to him, the truth into which the Holy Spirit leads us, and the life which he has come to give abundantly.

   Secular Franciscans should devote themselves especially to careful reading of the gospel, going from gospel to life and life to the gospel.

REFLECTION 5

God Is Love

Saint Francis never tired of speaking about God's goodness. He could not think of enough wonderful names to give him. Read slowly through this selection from the first Rule of Saint Francis:

"With our whole heart,
our whole soul,
our whole mind,
with our whole strength and fortitude
with our whole understanding
with all our powers
with every effort,
every affection,
every feeling,
every desire and wish
let us all love **the Lord God**
Who has given and gives to each one of us
our whole body, our whole soul and our whole life
. . .
let us desire nothing else,
let us want nothing else,
let nothing else please us and cause us delight
except our Creator, Redeemer and Savior,
the only true God,
Who is the fullness of good,
all good, every good, the true and supreme good,
Who alone is good,
merciful, gentle, delightful, and sweet,
Who alone is holy,
just, true, holy, and upright,
Who alone is kind, innocent, clean,
. . .
Wherever we are,
in every place,
at every hour,

at every time of the day,
every day and continually,
let all of us truly and humbly believe,
hold in our heart and love,
honor, adore, serve,
praise and bless,
glorify and exalt,
magnify and give thanks
to the Most High and Supreme Eternal God
Trinity and Unity,
Father, Son and Holy Spirit,
Creator of all,
Savior of all
Who believe and hope in Him...."

(*Saint Francis,* The Earlier Rule)

God Is Our Loving Parent

Above all, Francis thought of God as his good Father. In contemporary life, we may see God as a loving parent with the attributes of a loving father and a loving mother. (Often in this book we may refer to God as Father, as did Francis. That does not indicate any disrespect for the feminine image of God that is acknowledged today.) In Francis's rediscovery of Christ in the Gospel, he found that Christ continually called upon his Father, doing all things for love of his Father. Christ makes us his brothers and sisters. He gives us his own Father, the most loving parent!

God Is Good

God's goodness embodies the fundamental principle of Franciscan spirituality. This is the reason for all spiritual activity, the first and last answer for all problems. This is the idea that must move a Franciscan before any other idea. It is true, of course, that God is all-powerful, all-wise, all-knowing. He is Judge, Rewarder and Punisher. But Franciscan spirituality chooses to emphasize God's love and goodness.

God possesses all the goodness, beauty, happiness that the human mind can imagine—and infinitely more than we can envision. God is infinitely, eternally, unimaginably good. God is infinite love. And God wants us to share that goodness!

What Is Love?

It may be wise to stop here and consider this word "love." Love is the most precious thing in heaven and on earth. Love is of the very nature of God, and the prime commandment of human life. What is it?

Definitions are terribly unromantic, but let's try one anyway: To love someone is to want, to will, what is good for him or her. We say "want" and "will" instead of "give" because we may not be able actually to give someone what we would like. A mother can't give health to her dying baby; a friend can't actually give the gift of faith to another; sometimes we can't give away money because we don't have any ourselves. But in all these cases there can still be deep and generous love: We want our loved ones to have these things.

We can't always give people what they wish. We have to make a judgment as to what is really good. A mother does not let a child eat a half-gallon of ice cream simply because the child wants to gobble it up. A friend does not buy crack cocaine for someone or find him a mistress. Real love is not, however, "disciplinary" and authoritarian, imposing values on others.

Love gives what others need: physically, emotionally, spiritually, humanly. To love is to be alert and caring about others' needs, to be generous and unselfish in fulfilling them.

The greatest love has limits. In his earthly life, Christ could not be everywhere at once. He could only deal with people according to the time he had. Each of us has physical, emotional, intellectual and human limits. It is not unloving to pace yourself so that you can serve others many days, instead of exhausting all your resources on the first day. We are limited by obligations we already have. A wife cannot spend all her time taking care of people down the street when her own family needs her. A husband cannot fail to appear at work because his child wants to play ball with him.

Mother Teresa of Calcutta

Mother Teresa of Calcutta told how she brought food one day to a starving family. The mother excused herself for a little while. When she returned, Mother Teresa asked her what she had done. She had given half the food to another starving family.

While we must discuss these prosaic details about love, there is something about it that escapes the mold we try to put it in. Love is a sharing in God's own Spirit. There is something mysterious about it because it is divine. Love manifests itself in a myriad of ways which we notice when we are observant.

God is not bound by limitations. Hence the "wanting good" in the Trinity is boundless, infinite, total. God's love is an infinite torrent wider than the universe, flowing within the community called Father, Son and Spirit, and then pouring out on the whole world.

Jesus is the sign of this love, captured and emptied out into a body and spirit like ours. His love was divine—he gave us all he had, even his life. Yet his love was also human—even Jesus had to make judgments about what to give, when to give, what not to do, what was wise now, what tomorrow. He had to consider what others' needs really were and the best way to fill them.

But unless selfishness blankets it, love spreads like fire. Love simply must expand, radiating its light and warmth in all directions. The happier we are, the more we want to tell others, to share my happiness with them. God, who is Love itself, also wanted to share goodness with others. God was not "forced" to share this goodness; God wanted to! God wanted to be our Father, to give us divine life, goodness and happiness.

God's Greatest Gift of Love

The greatest thing God could give us was life—not only human life but a sharing in his own life. This mystery is called grace. Grace affects us at the very roots of our being. We are as new as the day we were first created. Yet the newness is not something "added" or laid on top of what we already are. It soaks our nature, permeates our being—if we let it. This means that the very power whereby God loves is our power. The very wisdom and intelligence with which God loves is ours. The very giving and going out, the generosity and feeling is all ours, for what is in God is in us, not by some kind of distant imitation but by our participation in God's own life.

Jesus showed us this life of grace that is God's love. He won for us our new creation through his own Spirit so that we can live the life of God in human form, as Jesus did. God did not give us Jesus "outside" of ourselves only—a man who lived two thousand years ago—or even the Risen Christ "up there" on the altar. God gives us himself, Jesus, his Spirit inside us as fire is inside wood without being the same as the wood.

If we let it, and in accord with our human limitations, we experience this new creation of our very being. No transforming power surpasses the power of love. A man or woman in love is a new person. So are we, if we let God's gracious gift of his own life soak into us.

The Franciscan Heart

We have said that the first emphasis of Franciscan spirituality is the realization that God is love. The second is that Christ is our brother in God's love, and we are all brothers and sisters in Christ. Francis rediscovered the plain truth of the Gospels: Christ is not only God; he is human. He is a true man with a real body, real mind, real will, real emotions, just like all his brothers and sisters, minus sin and the personal results of sin. Jesus, our brother, came that we might have life forever with God our Father.

The gospel life is simply to love as Jesus loved, as a human, knowing that it is God's love pulsing within us. The gospel life is to love people—not "people" in general, but *these* people, the ones we meet, the ones we live with or work with, the ones who may cause us difficulty or pain, as well as the ones who bring us joy. The Secular Franciscan Order offers me a particular community of people among whom we can be helped to experience and witness to this Francis- and Christ-like love.

God Is Love

We never forget the central theme: Behind it all, in it all, through it all, is the God who is love. Our response within all the everyday responses of daily life is: Blessed be God because he is good.

Questions for Reflection—What does "to love" mean? Do you see that there is mystery as well as everyday plainness about it? What is God's greatest gift to us?

Connecting With Scripture and Franciscan Writings—Christ's teachings and various reactions in Luke, Chapters 7-8. Bodo, pp. 14-17.

Application to Daily Life—What is your idea of love? Can you name the people who gave you your idea of love? What can God's parental love mean in your life? What is the greatest quality of a loving parent? Have you ever thought of Christ as your brother? How can you love him more? Try to realize and repeat often: "God is love. God is my loving parent. Christ is my brother. I want to love them and give them goodness in return."

Prayer—You are holy, Lord, the only God. You do wonders (Psalm 76:15).
> You are strong; You are great; You are the most high;
> You are the almighty King,
> You, Holy Father, the King of heaven and earth
> (John 17:11; Matthew 11:25).

> You are Three and One, Lord God of gods (cf. Psalm 135:2).
> You are good, all good, the highest good,
> Lord, God, living and true (cf. 1 Thessalonians 1:19).

> You are love, charity.
> You are wisdom; You are humility; You are patience
> (cf. Psalm 70:5);

> You are beauty; You are meekness; You are security;
> You are inner peace; You are joy; You are our hope and joy;
> You are justice; You are moderation; You are all our riches;
> (You are enough for us).
> You are beauty; You are meekness;

You are the protector (cf. Psalm 30:5).

You are our guardian and defender;
You are strength; You are refreshment (cf. Psalm 42:2).

You are our hope; You are our faith; You are our charity;
You are all our sweetness;
You are our eternal life:
Great and wonderful Lord,
God almighty, Merciful Savior.

(Ritual of the Secular Franciscan Order, p. 99)

From the Rule of the Secular Franciscan Order

PROLOGUE: Exhortation of Saint Francis
to the Brothers and Sisters in Penance
In the name of the Lord!
Concerning Those Who Do Penance

All who love the Lord with their whole heart, with their whole
soul and mind, with all their strength (cf. Mark 12:30), and
love their neighbors as themselves (cf. Matthew 22:39) and hate
their bodies with their vices and sins, and receive the Body
and Blood of our Lord Jesus Christ, and produce worthy fruits
of penance;

Oh, how happy and blessed are these men and women when
they do these things and persevere in doing them, because
"the spirit of the Lord will rest upon them" (cf. Isaiah 11:2)
and he will make "his home and dwelling among them"
(cf. John 14:23), and they are the sons of the heavenly Father
(cf. Matthew 5:45), whose works they do, and they are the
spouses, brothers, and mothers of our Lord Jesus Christ
(cf. Matthew 12:50).

We are spouses, when, by the Holy Spirit, the faithful soul is
united with our Lord Jesus Christ; we are brothers to him
when we fulfill "the will of the Father who is in heaven"
(Matthew 12:50).

We are mothers, when we carry him in our heart and body
(cf. 1 Corinthians 6:20) through divine love and a pure and
sincere conscience; we give birth to him through a holy life
which must give light to others by example (cf. Matthew 5:16).

Oh, how glorious it is to have a great and holy Father in
Heaven! Oh how glorious it is to have such a beautiful and
admirable Spouse, the Holy Paraclete!

Oh, how glorious it is to have such a Brother and such a Son, loved, beloved, humble, peaceful, sweet, lovable, and desirable above all: Our Lord Jesus Christ, who gave up his life for his sheep (cf. John 10:15) and prayed to the Father saying:

"O Holy Father, protect them with your name (cf. John 17:11) whom you gave me out of the world. I entrusted to them the message you entrusted to me, and they received it. They have known that in truth I came from you, they have believed that it was you who sent me. For these I pray, not for the world (cf. John 17:9). Bless and consecrate them, and I consecrate myself for their sakes. I do not pray for them alone; I pray also for those who will believe in me through their word (cf. John 17:20) that they may be holy by being one as we are (cf. John 17:11). And I desire, Father, to have them in my company where I am to see this glory of mine in your kingdom" (cf. John 17:6-24).

Christ, the Masterpiece Planned From Eternity

"He is the image of the invisible God, the firstborn of all creation; for in him all things were created.... He himself is before all things."
—Colossians 1:15-17

Imagine the eternal God being able to express all his love in a single gift: infinite, eternal, unspeakable life and love concentrated in an individual being. That gift is Jesus.

God "had," we say, an eternal plan. That plan was to share himself with intelligent, free, loving beings whom he would create not just as beings who are somewhat "like" God because they can think and love and act, but persons who love with the power of God's love, judge with the wisdom of God, love not just with human life, but with a sharing of divine life itself which possesses their being.

Christ the Eternal Masterpiece

God's plan is centered in Jesus. Jesus is the eternal model of all God's children. God "thought" of him first, as the center of all creation.

Through Jesus, divine life would be given to all his brothers and sisters. He is the source through whom divine life lives in a human body and thence flows to every human being on earth. All things were made in him, through him, and for him. He is the First Adorer, the Perfect Child, the Model Creature, the "firstborn of all creation" and the firstborn of many brothers and sisters.

God the Eternal Son, at one point in time, became God made man. But every creature before and after him, the first to the last man and woman on earth, was made in his image, destined to be saved by him, drawn to God through him. He is "the meeting place of uncreated and created love."

Images of the Masterpiece

Christ is the image of God, but God had in mind countless images of Christ. Mary, the Mother to be, was the first of these. Then came all the other brothers and sisters of Christ, every human being on earth.

Whether a man or woman knows Christ or will ever hear of Christ, he or she is saved by Christ, loved by Christ, called to Christ. If our first parents are with God, it is because they were saved by the death and Resurrection of Christ.

The Tragedy of Sin

Only one real calamity occurred in all human history. That is sin, man's cutting himself off from God's plan. Mankind threw away its relationship with God and turned to being self-sufficient, self-centered, attempting to find redemption apart from God's plan.

Christ the Redeemer

The children of mankind are consequently born as members of the human race that abandoned God, an alienated people. But the remedy for this tragedy already surrounds every baby who is born, for the plan of God sweeps on.

The redeeming grace of Christ is offered to every human being on earth because every one belongs to Christ. Each one is called to be healed and raised up to share the life and victory of Jesus, the First Man. The Masterpiece, the Head and Source of creation, is its redeemer. The model for all men is the model for those who must suffer the blight of sin on their lives. Jesus emptied himself, entering into our life as it has been damaged by sin. Without sin himself, and without the moral effects of sin, he nevertheless experienced the sinful condition of the world. Ultimately this power of evil killed him, but because he forgave sin and trusted his Father, Jesus rose to a new and eternal life. He can now give that life to his brothers and sisters with a power that cannot be stopped. His Spirit lives in us. Therefore, we are able to conquer sin and death with his power.

Christ the King

By the "failure" of his death, Jesus becomes the irresistible destroyer of sin and giver of life. He has power: gentle but infinite, divine but humanly channeled. He is King. His law is the Spirit within us. His kingdom is grace. His punishment is forgiveness. His power is humility. His treasure is love. Saint Francis was thrilled with this great and simple idea of Christ at the center of creation, not only as God but as the man who became the world's Victim, Priest and King. The great victory of the Resurrection meant that evil is destroyed forever and death has lost its sting. Francis saw himself as the "Herald of the Great King." A herald is one who comes with a message from a king. Francis came singing the Good News from the King of Kings: God is love; Christ is our Brother who gives us life, saves us, and brings us to the Kingdom of the Good God. Every action we perform, therefore, must somehow be an act of loyal love for the King.

Questions for Reflection—Why did God will the creation of the world? Who is God's eternal Masterpiece? Why? Who are images of the Masterpiece? What did Saint Francis call himself?

Connecting With Scripture and Franciscan Writings—The apostles and the Bread of Life in Matthew, Chapter 13; Mark, Chapter 6; John, Chapter 6. Bodo, pp. 1-19.

Application to Daily Life—If Christ is the center and meaning of everything, can you apply this to everyday life? For instance: Should you go to this movie or not? Should you marry this person or not? Should you say what you are thinking or not? Everything depends on "What does our Lord want in this matter now?" Devotion to the King means loyalty, generosity, courage in the daily business of living and thinking and loving. Every moment of life has reference to Christ. Consider this often. Pray each day: "Blessed is He who comes as King, in the name of the Lord! Peace in heaven, and glory in the highest!"

Prayer—We adore you, Lord Jesus Christ, here and in all your churches in the whole world, and we bless you, because by your holy cross you have redeemed the world. Amen (Normile, *Every Day and All Day*, p. 105).

From the Rule of the Secular Franciscan Order

5. Secular Franciscans, therefore, should seek to encounter the living and active person of Christ in their brothers and sisters, in Sacred Scripture, in the Church, and in liturgical activity. The faith of Saint Francis, who often said, "I see nothing bodily of the Most High Son of God in this world except his most holy body and blood," should be the inspiration and pattern of their eucharistic life.

REFLECTION 7

The Grace of Christ

"I came so that they might have life and have it more abundantly."
—John 10:10

A Different Kind of Life

Saint Peter came a long way. From being the impulsive, undependable and uncomprehending friend of Christ, he became the apostle who could write down one of the most amazing and mysterious sentences in all literature: "[God] has given us his precious and very great promises, so that through them you may escape from the corruption that is in the world because of lust and may become participants of the divine nature" (2 Peter 1:4).

It is easy to become technical in talking about grace, as if it were a "something" to be analyzed like calcium in our bones or red corpuscles in our blood. We easily fall into the jargon of the business world, speaking of "having" grace as if it were a bottom-line item to be tallied or the deed to six downtown blocks in Chicago, and of trying to "get more grace" like squirrels gathering nuts for a long winter.

This language is understandable, but it is misleading nevertheless. We don't use it in ordinary life because the inexactness would be immediately evident. A wife doesn't bake a special pie to "get more grace" from her husband. And (unless there's a poor relationship) he doesn't consider himself in a "state of marriage" with her, as something merely official, settled-once-for-all, static as a statue and only a little more lively.

Grace Is Free

"Grace" means free, gratis. In a sense, we can say that everything God gives us is freely given, for we certainly can't earn it. But the special "gratis-ness" of grace is that it's so special we wouldn't even have thought of it.

If God makes a tree, it is natural for us to expect that there will be ground, sunlight and rain. That goes with "tree." So also, when we look at human nature, it is natural for us to expect that if man is to think, he has to have something to think with. If he's free, he has to possess the power to make decisions. If he has a physical being, he has to have what a physical being needs to live—the processes of the body. But we don't expect either a tree or a man to have anything beyond what is tree-y and human. We don't expect a tree to be able to walk over to the post office just as we don't expect a Shetland pony to compose a symphony.

What is it we don't expect of a human being, even in our richest imaginings? What, for man, is like a tree wanting to pray, or your dog deciding to give up Alpo during Lent?

The unexpected gift is the grace to live on God's level: not to *be* God but to have God's life—not just glorious, intelligent, free human life, but God's kind of decision-making, God's unconditional loving and God's way of living.

Our Need for Grace

A dog, no matter how devoted, cannot communicate with a man in any of the same ways that a woman can communicate with her husband (though some wives may debate this). So also, for all our glorious human gifts, we could no more look upon the face of God, speak to God directly, think God's thoughts, love with love as perfect as God's, than the most "intelligent" dog in the world would write a sonnet to another dog.

These are earthy comparisons, perhaps too gross. But we need to be impressed with the divine gift that our Father has given us in Jesus. To our nature—all that would be expected to belong to a normal human being—God joins his own life. This is the most "gracious" act possible— the freest of all free gifts.

Actually, there never was a "natural" man or woman. From eternity God planned to make us his real children with his own life in us, not just a natural life. Maybe it's because we've had this special calling that we sometimes think we have a right to it—as if it were part of our nature.

So much for the necessary distinctions. When we try to realize what this gracious gift is, we had best take the words of Jesus: "[B]ecause I live, you also will live. On that day you will know that I am in my Father, and you in me, and I in you. They who have my command- ments and keep them are those who love me; and those who love me will be loved by my Father.... Those who love me will keep my word, and my Father will love them; and we will come to them and make our home with them" (John 14). "I am the vine, you are the branches. Those who abide in me and I in them bear much fruit" (John 15:5). "If you...know how to give good gifts to your children, how much more will the heavenly Father give the Holy Spirit to those who ask him" (Luke 11:13).

Grace and God's Plan

We begin to realize that grace is what the Bible is about—all that God eternally wanted to give us, the reason Christ became man, the purpose of his sending his Spirit within us. God raises us up to himself and we are his friends.

Grace, then, refers to the relationship of love between God and his children. It is "something" in the sense that we are changed to the roots of our being when God recreates us. It's as if God were to make a statue out of nothing and then were to recreate the statue into a beautiful human being.

Grace is not "something" in the sense of one pancake plopped on top of another (a faulty way of illustrating the fact that "grace builds on nature"). Our life is graced. It has a divine quality put there by God.

God always wants to deepen and enrich this quality in us. He is constantly calling us to be open to his presence so that we can more and more be possessed with the vision he has of the world, with the boundless love with which he cares for all his creatures, with the power that no other power can withstand.

Grace and Everyday Living

Individual graces are not really separate from this one great relationship of God though we do speak of "actual" grace, the grace to act. This means that the same divine life that permeates our being is available for the individual actions whereby we live that life. Indeed this grace to act can come before the full divine life, as when a sinner begins to be drawn to conversion and accepts God's love.

"Everything is grace!" Saint Paul said. We must constantly try to understand our relationship with God as the very heart of our life. Grace is not, on the one hand, a sort of mechanical ticket to heaven lodged somewhere in the back of our soul. Nor, on the other hand, is it a gimmick that will take us to heaven without entering into our consciousness, our decisions, our everyday actions.

When Michelangelo finished his famous statue of Moses, it looked so lifelike that he was tempted to shout to it "Speak!" What Michelangelo could not do, God can. He took a part of his earth and said "Jesus!" And Jesus, having given his human gift back to God in trustful death, now says to all his brothers and sisters, "Awake! Believe the Good News. I am the life."

Questions for Reflection—What does Saint Peter say about the Christian life? What does "grace" mean literally? What is the best way of describing grace? What would you say instead of "getting more grace"?

Connecting With Scripture and Franciscan Writings—Suffering to come, transfiguration, and love of God in Luke, Chapters 9-10; Mark, Chapter 9. Bodo, pp. 20-22.

Application to Daily Life—Millions of people may perform similar actions, but what makes their actions unique? Life is movement. We move with Christ's power. Some choose to move with only their own power. Try to be conscious of God's sanctifying power in your life. Sanctifying means making holy, making sacred, consecrating. What difference should sanctifying grace make to your work or play, meeting others, the married or single life, suffering? Nothing else in life really matters than that we grow in God's life. Thank God for this gift.

Prayer—Oh, God, it overwhelms me to think that you live in me. What an awesome God you are to come to one like me. Enable me to yield my will to your grace each moment of my life. Amen.

REFLECTION 8

Jesus Visible Today

"By her relationship with Christ, the Church is a kind of sacrament or sign of intimate union with God, and of the unity of all mankind. She is also the instrument for the achievement of such union and unity."

—*"Dogmatic Constitution on the Church," No. 1*

"It is of the essence of the Church that she be both human and divine, visible and yet invisibly endowed, eager to act and yet devoted to contemplation, present in this world and yet not at home in it."

—*"Constitution on the Sacred Liturgy," No. 2*

The Word Made Flesh

Jesus is the Word made flesh. He is God made visible. He is God showing himself in human terms. He is, in the words that form the title of a famous book, "the sacrament of the encounter with God."

God adapted himself to our way of communicating—that is, by sight, hearing, touch, taste and smell. Jesus was something people could "handle" as Saint John says. They could see him, hear him, touch him. If Jesus spoke to you, God spoke. If he forgave you, God forgave you. He is, therefore, a sacrament; rather, the sacrament of God.

Now, God's communication of himself was to go on after Jesus' death. But the risen Jesus is no longer visible, audible, touchable. So he left another sacrament like himself. Not just one body, but a Body formed by many bodies, many persons—the followers of Christ. Until the end of time the Church is the "sign" or "sacrament" or "visibility" of Christ. The Church bears the terrible burden and the glory of saying to the world, "If you want to see and hear the love and forgiveness of Jesus, look at us, listen to us."

Through this weak and wonderful, glorious and humiliated "Body" Jesus acts today. "Not many of you were wise or noble when you were first called," said Saint Paul to his Corinthian parish. Yet that is what God chooses to use as his continuing self-communication, the ongoing redemptive work of Jesus until the end of time.

Mankind always seems to itch to have some kind of super-church:

pure, entirely "spiritual," untouched by structure, organization, human weakness, limitation, weakness and sin. But such an unreal dream forgets the nature of man. We are body-people. We are human only if we are whole: spirit expressing itself bodily.

God not only emptied himself in becoming man. He continues the "hiding" of his divine glory beneath the unlikely form of a body of people called Christians, united by his Spirit and diverse as their many temperaments, cultures and histories.

Loyalty to the Church

Many reformers existed in Saint Francis's day and every one of them had a real complaint. Many of the clergy were not worthy of the name. Wealth was a bigger factor in Church life than Jesus ever would have wished. The Church really needed a reform in its "heads," the clergy, if not in its head, the pope. Most of these reforms were shipwrecked on the rocks of their own rebelliousness. They tried to impose a reform on the Church from without. They would cure the Church if they had to kill it in the process. But Francis—who could spot a greedy priest or hypocritical bishop as well as anyone else—preserved a pure and simple reverence for all priests and a loyal obedience to the pope that many today would call "unenlightened." If God were going to do any good for his Church through Francis, Francis believed He would do it within the structure of the Church.

Francis saw the mystery of the Church: new wine in new wineskins, divine life pulsing through arteries sometimes clogged with spiritual cholesterol, her healing of the world hampered because her hands had become weak or arthritic.

But this is the Church that exists; a body of people united in Jesus, breathing his love into the world, perpetuating his death and Resurrection—but in the glorious and inglorious ups and downs of everyday human life.

The Mystical Body of Christ

The faults of the Church are evident. What we need is a constant reminder of the divine glory within the Church. Saint Paul compared the Church to a human body: "For just as the body is one and has many members, and all the members of the body, though many, are one body, so it is with Christ.... Now you are the body of Christ, and individually members of it" (1 Corinthians 12:12, 27).

Saint Paul's main emphasis is on the unity of the body in being and charity, through the gift of the one Spirit. It is the oneness in charity and truth that is primary. The plurality of gifts, the pluralism of opinions and practices is possible only in a unity of Christlike charity expressing itself loyally within the imperfect structure of the visible Body.

Jesus himself spoke of the vine and the branches. There is one vine, one source of life. One root and stock provides the life and fruit of all the branches: us, the many members who have been grafted on by the free gift of God's grace.

The members of any organization within the Church must always see that group and its purpose as absolutely subordinate to the life and mission of the Church. To be a Franciscan is to follow Francis in trying to lead the gospel life where Francis lived it: within the Church, that inefficient and ridiculous pilgrim walking the way of the cross yet already alive with the life of the risen Christ.

Questions for Reflection—How is Jesus a "sacrament" of God? How is the Church itself a sacrament? How is tension between the "spirit" of the Church and its visible structure a healthy one? Will the Mystical Body of Christ be ideal some day in history? Explain.

Connecting With Scripture and Franciscan Writings—God's love and human hypocrisy in Matthew, Chapter 10; Luke, Chapters 11-12. Bodo, pp. 22-24.

Application to Daily Life—How do you believe you are important as a member of the Body of Christ? Why are you necessary? What can you do to make the structure of the Church more convincing and attractive in your parish? What temptations to a purely "spiritual" Church or fraternity do you have? Think of three specific things to do on a regular basis to benefit the whole Body of Christ.

Prayer—Lord Jesus, as a member of the body of Christ, I can be your hand to help another, your voice to praise God, your heart to love the Church into wholeness. Praise you, Jesus, for making me a part of your Body. Please show me how to use this precious gift to help "thy Kingdom come." Amen.

From the Rule of the Secular Franciscan Order

3. The present rule, succeeding "Memoriale Propositi" (1221) and the rules approved by the Supreme Pontiffs Nicholas IV and Leo XIII, adapts the Secular Franciscan Order to the needs and expectations of the Holy Church in the conditions of changing times. Its interpretation belongs to the Holy See, and its application will be made by the General Constitutions and particular statutes.

REFLECTION 9

The Real Christ

"O Lord Jesus Christ, I entreat you to give me two graces before I die: First, that in my lifetime I may feel in body and soul as far as possible the pain You endured, dear Lord, in the hour of Your most bitter suffering; and second, that I may feel in my heart as far as possible that excess of love by which You, O Son of God, were inflamed to undertake so cruel a suffering for us sinners."

—*Little Flowers of Saint Francis*

Saint Francis's Two Loves

In front of the altar of the friary chapel of Greccio, Italy, you can still see the large stone, with a V-like hollow on top, which Saint Francis used as his Christmas crib, thereby popularizing a devotion we still have today.

The crib and the cross were the two loves of Jesus' life—the mystery of the Incarnation of the eternal God and the mystery of his giving up of that life.

True Man

Christians have been so busy proving that Jesus is God that they have sometimes de-emphasized the fact that he is man, truly human, with all the feelings and experiences, joys and sorrows of our human life. When we said that he had no sin or any personal result of sin, we somehow felt that he was exempt from emotion, temptation, limitation, problems.

The baby in the crib of Bethlehem is a statement of the goodness of human life. "God doesn't make junk," as the old cliché says. It was as if God said, "Do you doubt the goodness of what I have created? I will enter into it *as it is*. Not only as it is damaged by sin, but *as it is human*."

The baby Francis saw in the crib would grow like any other baby, since Christ would not have been a true human being if he had never been faced with the need of depending on others for care, of making up his mind, of choosing freely, or taking one course rather than another—at a time when both looked good. When he prayed, his knees felt the hard ground beneath his bones like anyone else's. When he drank wine,

33

it exhilarated his body and spirit like anyone else's. He knew the courage and discipline required to get up and go to work every day. When frustration or failure fell on his path, he had to exercise patience like anyone else. People ignored him, misjudged him, slandered him and finally killed him. It cost him the same effort of courage, trust in his Father, forgiveness that these things cost us every day.

He sensed who he was, but this knowledge need not have been sharp and clear. He was appointed Messiah from eternity, but the Jewish boy and young man had to learn, by prayer and openness, that the real path of the Messiah was in the suffering servant of Isaiah. When he faced death, he cried out in terror just as we do. And when he put his life into the hands of his Father, the gift was made in the dark. Certainly his Father had said he would raise him up: He says the same to us. But the passing to the Father was nevertheless an act of trust made in the darkness.

Jesus didn't give us any new things to do. He simply revealed the Kingdom of God within life as it is: beautiful, growing, hoping, loving, forgiving human life.

The One Holiness

Vatican II emphasized the fact that we all are called to holiness, whether we are priest or salesman, teenager or aged nun, bartender or Trappist monk, president or homeless woman. That holiness is the result of receiving of God's life by faith and love into our life as it is.

All the goodness in the world is God's goodness. Better said, the world is full of God's goodness. Our task is to see it shining there, allow it to possess us, to treasure it and share the vision with others.

The Cross

The other great emphasis in Francis's life was the crucified Christ. The actual physical sufferings of Christ were a constant object of his meditation. The literal-minded poet saw the hard facts: It's what you put on the line that shows how dedicated you are. Jesus held nothing back. He deliberately walked into Jerusalem knowing what would happen to him. He experienced not a quick, easy plunge into unconsciousness by a sword thrust but the long agony of the cross. Jesus wanted to swallow, as it were, all the misery that sin had brought into the world. He let it fill him, possess him in the same way that he wanted to possess others by love. He let it ruin all his plans, scare away his friends, and finally destroy him.

But sinful men had not counted on one thing: being forgiven. Jesus destroyed the power of sinful men by forgiving them. When they did their worst, he did his best. At the heart of salvation are three words, "Father, forgive them."

Contemplating the birth of Jesus and his crucifixion brought Francis to the boundaries of joy and sadness. Francis would be so exhilarated at the beauty of the Incarnation that he would take two sticks and act as if he were playing the violin, praising God in song. Pondering the painful suffering of Jesus' crucifixion would cause Francis to cry agonizing tears of compassion for his suffering Savior.

The Christian Life

We follow Saint Francis in the divine "ups and downs" of life. Every day is "up"—letting the vision of faith see the beauty of God's love saving the world, letting him reveal the world of the human Christ. Every day is "down"—giving up a selfish use of that world by dying to selfishness in all its disguises: dying to revenge and greediness, cruelty and lust, laziness and bossiness. Thereby we live through another "up"—another rising with Christ to richer, deeper, more joyful companionship with him. Death and resurrection every day is as prosaic as Nazareth, painful as Calvary, glorious as Easter morning.

Questions for Reflection—What particular activities in your life can you see Jesus experiencing if he walked the earth today in bodily form? If there is only one holiness in the Church, what is the difference between people? What is daily dying and rising?

Connecting With Scripture and Franciscan Writings—Penance and forgiveness in Luke, Chapters 13-15; John, Chapter 10. Bodo, pp. 24-26.

Application to Daily Life—Think of yourself as one who shares in the holiness of God. How does this view of yourself affect your choices and daily activity? Choose three actions each day to do deliberately and joyfully in union with Christ. Visualize yourself walking and talking with Jesus as you carry out these actions.

Prayer—Help me, Lord, to seek you in all the events of my life, to praise you in good times and in troubled moments. Enable me to bear the crosses of my life as you bore yours—with courage and with faith. Amen.

REFLECTION 10

The Gift of the Spirit

"Then he entered into the city of Assisi and began, as though drunk with the Holy Spirit, to praise God aloud in the streets and the squares."

The earliest biography thus describes Francis's actions after he had stripped himself of everything in the world—even his clothing, which he had laid at the feet of his angry and bewildered father. Now he was free and the Spirit within him found no obstacle to complete possession.

Another early biographer describes Francis's reaction when at Mass he heard the words of Christ about having neither gold nor silver, scrip nor bread, neither shoes nor two garments. Francis, he says, was "seized" by the Holy Spirit and joyfully cried out, "This is what I want; this is what I seek; this I will do with all my heart!"

The Full Gift: Pentecost

The Holy Spirit is not an "extra" in Christian holiness. Rather, the sending of the Spirit is the completing of the entire beautiful plan of God to share his Life with us. Jesus, the second person of the Trinity, "emptied himself" and took our human nature. As our brother, he let himself be possessed fully by the Spirit. The Spirit "powered" him through a human life like ours, led him into a loving sacrificial death. Because Jesus emptied himself totally in trust and love, he could be raised in victory to the eternal glory he had with the Father and the Spirit. But now—and only now, after his death—could the victorious God-man Savior send his Spirit, the Spirit of the Father, to complete his work on earth.

The Spirit thus takes the place of the "absent" Jesus. We know very well that Jesus is not really "absent." The word refers to the fact that his visible and mortal life is over. All that he came to do can now be made available to all people through his Spirit. The Spirit flows out upon the whole world, as it were, through the pierced heart of Christ.

Only because he suffered could Jesus release the Spirit in this way. "[I]f I do not go away, the Advocate will not come to you" (John 16:7). "...[N]o one can enter the kingdom of God without being born of water and the Spirit" (John 3:5).

36

The Gift

The Rite of Confirmation has these words at the actual conferring of the sacrament: "Receive the seal of the Holy Spirit, the Gift of the Father." We can never emphasize enough that the Spirit is *the* gift God wanted to give from eternity. All that is said about grace, about God's love, about God's eternal plan is summed up in the Spirit—God's gift—himself. There is but one revelation, or self-communicating, of God. It comes from the Father through the Son and is completed by the Spirit to the glory of the Father and the Son.

These are unfathomable mysteries. We cannot hope to have this mysterious action of God neatly blueprinted in human sentences. But neither should we restrain our minds and hearts from *experiencing* as much as possible the infinitely tender coming of God by his Spirit. God is love, and the Spirit is God's love as gift to us.

I Have Come That You May Have Life

The Spirit makes us alive, really alive, fully alive as God intended us to be. By opening ourselves to God's offer of himself—our ability to respond is itself his gift—our being is gradually transformed. God's way of loving becomes our way of loving if we allow the Spirit to possess us. God's way of seeing is the way of our own mind unless we let selfishness darken it. We move into deeper understanding of God's ways, greater experience of his loving presence and power in our lives, because "God's love has been poured into our hearts through the Holy Spirit that has been given to us" (Romans 5:5). The whole visible Body of the Church, as well as our own body-person, is a temple of the Holy Spirit. In spite of suffering, weariness, problems, temptation and even daily faults, the Spirit produces in us a *conviction* of his presence and power. We experience the power of his acting in us if we allow him. We gradually realize that our immersion into water at Baptism was an immersion into God's life. In short, we know when we are in Christ because then we let truth and love possess us. We realize that this way of being is God's way.

The Gifts of the Spirit

Only as people possessed by the Spirit can we rightly estimate the individual gifts of the Spirit. We are made to give glory to God as his children gathered together. Every gift of the Spirit is given for this purpose—our ability to pray, to love and to forgive, to work and to wait, to suffer patiently and to fight valiantly, to walk in the valley of darkness or skip along the mountaintops.

There is a particular kind of gift which the Spirit gives the Church to make it visible and credible as the "holy people of God" and in this way to complete the work done by the officials of the Church. The forms taken by these "charismata" cannot be foreseen (wisdom, knowledge, miracles, discerning of spirits, gifts of government, prophecy, tongues) but must constantly be re-discovered and gratefully accepted. "The wind blows where it chooses, and you hear the sound of it, but you do not know where it comes from or where it goes. So it is with everyone who is born of the Spirit" (John 3:8). Vatican II said, "Extraordinary gifts are not to be rashly sought after, nor are the fruits of apostolic labor to be presumptuously expected from them." At the same time, the bishops said, we should remember that there are the "more simple and widely diffused" gifts, to be received with thanksgiving and consolation. Our very life is gift. Everything we are able to do that is good involves the gift of grace. Our part is to be as open and transparent as possible to whatever the Spirit wishes to effect in us.

The Franciscan Charism

The movement toward gospel poverty in the Middle Ages was an example of a special charism or gift of the Spirit for the ever-needed renewal of the Church. Saint Francis was gifted with a special charism to be a prominent part of the renewal of the Church of his day. We now open ourselves to all the Spirit wishes to do for the Church today through the continuing spirit of Francis.

We are called to be a community of brothers and sisters under one Father, bound together for the sake of Christ and through his love, brothers and sisters in the Spirit.

Saint Francis wished to make an addition to the final Rule of 1223. He wanted to say that the Holy Spirit is the true "Minister General," or "Superior" of the whole Order. The canon lawyers patiently explained to him that once the Pope had approved the Rule, no changes could be made.

The Spirit is our first "Superior" nevertheless.

Questions for Reflection—What phrase or word best expresses your experience of the Holy Spirit? What should the Spirit produce in your life? How do you recognize the gifts of the Spirit in your life?

Connecting With Scripture and Franciscan Writings—The gifts of the Spirit, particularly the gift of love in 1 Corinthians, Chapters 12, 13, 14. Bodo, pp. 27-30.

Application to Daily Life—What is the biggest obstacle in your life to being open to the Spirit? What needs of others is the Spirit calling you to recognize and fulfill? What fruits of the Spirit do you see in the Church and world today? Try to pay deliberate attention to the Spirit in one prayer, one conversation, one piece of work each day.

Prayer—Spirit of the living God, I am yours. Fill me with your wondrous gifts of love and kindness and wisdom. Use me to witness to your presence in my little corner of the world. Amen.

REFLECTION 11

Mary, Our Mother and Model

"Hail, O Lady!
Holy Queen,
. . .
Hail, His Palace!
Hail, His Tabernacle!
Hail, His Dwelling!
Hail, His Robe!
Hail, His Servant!
Hail, His Mother!"

—Saint Francis, Prayer to the Blessed Mother

Mary and Christ

As we have seen, the human nature of Christ was God's eternal master-piece. Next in his beautiful plan was Mary. She would receive fullness of grace through Christ. Christ was the new Adam. He alone could save the human race. It was Adam who lost our inheritance of grace. But just as the first Adam had an Eve at his side, so the New Adam, Christ, has at his side a new Eve, Mary. She could not save us, but Christ allowed her to cooperate in his saving work.

Mary Is Truly Our Mother

Mary gave birth to Christ at Bethlehem. But as soon as Christ began to live on earth, his Body began to live, too—the vine and the branches. Mary gladly said "yes" to Christ's coming—therefore to the coming of the Mystical Body. She is the mother of all who would have life in Christ.

Christ gave her to us as mother. She deliberately and gladly con-sented to the litany of sorrows that was needed to open our Father's house for us. When she spoke her bridal consent to God, she said, "Be it done to me according to thy word." At that moment she also consented to become mother to all the children of God in that mysterious, eternal kingdom of which the angel spoke. Mary as mother is the most under-standable image of what God's love is for us. If every mother loves her child, how warmly must the perfect mother love her Child and her chil-

40

dren! And this love can only be a reflection of the infinite love of the Father for his children.

Franciscan Love for Mary

A deep and abiding love for Mary, the mother of Christ and our spiritual mother, is a characteristic mark of the Franciscan Order. Saint Francis's devotion centered around one fact: Mary gave us our Brother, Christ, and shared his poverty. She was always to be a special advocate and protectress of the Order. The Constitutions fix this love in Secular Franciscan life by stating: "Mary, Mother of Jesus, is the model of listening to the Word and of faithfulness to vocation: we, like Francis, see all the gospel virtues realized in her.... The Secular Franciscans and their Fraternities should seek to live the experience of Francis, who made the Virgin the guide of his activity. With her, like the disciples at Pentecost, they should welcome the Spirit to create a community of love" (Article 16).

Saint Francis himself prayed to her before each hour of the Office:

"Holy Virgin Mary, there is none like unto you born in the world among women, daughter and handmaid of the most high King, the heavenly Father! Mother of our most holy Lord Jesus Christ, spouse of the Holy Spirit, pray for us with Saint Michael the Archangel and all the virtues of heaven and all the saints, to your most holy, beloved Son, our Lord and Master. Amen."

Mother of the Franciscan Order

The cradle of the Franciscan Order was the Portiuncula ("The Little Portion"), the poor little church outside Assisi which was dedicated to Our Lady of the Angels. It was no accident that this greatest of mothers should stand again at a poor cradle. To Francis, Portiuncula was a royal castle, like that other one at Bethlehem, for poverty was the badge of the noble children of God. He said, "Poverty is a royal virtue, because it shone so brightly in the King and Queen" (Celano, *The Life of Saint Francis*).

Mary, Our Teacher

Like all good mothers, Mary teaches us. Above all, she teaches us humility. Humility, the sister of poverty in the mind of Saint Francis, is nowhere more beautifully expressed than in the song of Mary, the Magnificat. It is the soft overture to the Sermon on the Mount and its heart-thought: "Blessed are the poor in spirit." Mary was humble in recognizing her complete unworthiness before God. She trusted confidently in the perfect love of God always eager to lift his creatures up to divine childhood and perfect joy.

The Franciscan Crown

One way Secular Franciscans honor Mary is by saying the Crown of the Seven Joys of Mary (the Franciscan Rosary). Saint Francis's great emphasis on joy is reflected in this devotion begun by one of his followers. We are all in a "vale of tears." We need to share Mary's joy. Perhaps the following thoughts on the Seven Joys will help us when we say this rosary:

1) **The Annunciation.** Mary's joy springs from her deep humility. "He looked down kindly on the lowliness of His handmaid." "Be it done to me according to thy word."

2) **The Visitation.** The joy of Mary's charity blooms as she hastens to help Elizabeth. No sooner does she possess Christ than she begins to share him with others.

3) **The Birth of Our Lord.** Mary's joy in the Divine riches from heaven is now possessed by poor human beings on earth. The joy of poverty lies in seeing where true riches lie.

4) **The Adoration of the Magi.** The joy of Mary extends to the Gentiles also (we ourselves!) who will be the newly adopted children of God.

5) **The Finding in the Temple.** Mary experiences the joy of finding Christ again, she in innocence and we in penance, all of us in prayer and charity.

6) **Appearance of Christ to Mary After the Resurrection.** The joy of Mary's faith blooms when her strong faith on Calvary is rewarded.

7) **The Assumption and Coronation.** The joy of her hope is fulfilled even beyond her expectations. "The eye has not seen, nor the ear heard...."

Mary's Help

Mary helps us grow in Christ: 1) Because she is a perfect image of God's love; 2) Because she loves us as a true mother; 3) Because she leads us in her way of humility; 4) Because she encourages us in prayer, by her joy even in suffering.

Questions for Reflection—How is Mary our mother? Why is Mary the Mother of the Franciscan Order? What virtue does Mary especially teach us? What is the Franciscan Crown?

Connecting With Scripture and Franciscan Writings—the Kingdom becomes more evident in Luke, Chapters 17-18; John, Chapter 11. Bodo, pp. 30-33.

Application to Daily Life—Learn to see the value of a deep devotion to Mary in your personal life. Many of your problems will disappear. For example, Mary's joys coexisted with suffering. How can you find joy even in the sufferings and problems of daily life? Pray the Franciscan Crown at least once this week. Say it with reverence. Decide whether or not it will become a daily or weekly practice for you.

Prayer—Holy Mary, Mother of God, you trusted God with your whole life when you said, "Let it be done to me." Show us how to give birth to Jesus in a world so in need of his love and forgiveness. Amen.

From the Rule of the Secular Franciscan Order

9. The Virgin Mary, humble servant of the Lord, was open to his every word and call. She was embraced by Francis with indescribable love and declared the protectress and advocate of his family. The Secular Franciscans should express their ardent love for her by imitating her complete self-giving and by praying earnestly and confidently.

Conversion

*I*f we are to turn our lives to God, we must
change. Change can be difficult and painful.
Giving up old ways is challenging, especially
when we have considered "the way we've always
done it" to be "right." The process of spiritual
change is conversion. Conversion is not a once
and for all experience. Rather it is something
we do daily for the rest of our lives because
while we still breathe, we do not reach the
spiritual perfection to which God calls us.
The following reflections invite you to
conversion again and again and again....

REFLECTION 12

Penance: Turning to God and Away From Sin

"Fear God, love God, convert yourself from bad to good."
—Saint Francis, from Jorgensen, Life of St. Francis

We can react in two ways to the beautiful truths we have been studying. First, we can feel a deep sense of joy and security in the fact that God our Father and Mother loves us more than any father and mother ever loved a child; that Christ our Brother continues his human-divine life in our human-graced life; and that the Spirit of love dwells within us to be our strength, our consolation and our light.

We can respond, at the same time, with a frank and genuine sense of sorrow for the indifference, selfishness and sinful attitude with which we have repaid God's love in the past and even in the present. If we have not turned completely away from God by mortal sinfulness, we have nevertheless been guilty of persistent attitudes of neglect and self-centeredness. We have shown a certain unwillingness to love God "all the way." Selfishness toward others has resulted.

Both attitudes, sorrow and joy, are part of the Christian virtue of penance.

What Is Penance?

The word "penance" is used in several meanings which we should clearly distinguish. First, it refers to a total turning to God by a basic act of faith, sorrow and love that becomes our *way of life*. This is what our Lord was referring to in his first recorded public words: "Repent, for the kingdom of heaven is at hand," [Matthew 5:17]. We will refer to this kind of penance as *conversion*. The only way anyone can turn from evil and choose good is through the deep realization of God's love which calls us to live so much in the awareness of his loving presence that there is no appeal in evil for us, because it is not any part of God. In returning God's love, we can only choose the ways that are of God.

Second, the word "penance" refers to practices of self-discipline and

46

self-control: things like giving up candy or cigarettes during Lent, getting up regularly for Mass, forming the habit of moderation in food, drink, entertainment, in general saying "no" to certain things not strictly necessary and "yes" to certain other things when they are not strictly required. These penances enable us to say "no" or "yes" when we really must.

It should be obvious that the value of this kind of penance depends very much on how much we have entered into the first kind of penance. This second kind of penance we will call *self-discipline*.

A third kind of penance is that which sees the damage done by sin and the perfect atonement made by Christ in his life, death and Resurrection. It joins this reparation of Christ, knowing that there is no other conceivable way to "make up" for the past. We will call this *Christian atonement*.

Finally, there is the "penance" that is part of the Sacrament of Reconciliation. It can include all three kinds just mentioned.

Penance as Conversion

Saint Francis speaks of a time when "he was still in sin." He is referring to the time of his life before he "caught on" to what the Christian life was all about. Like many others—indeed, it should happen to all of us—he went through a "conversion." The word means a total turn-around, doing a "180," a complete giving of self to Christ, a conscious, all-out surrender to the grace of God.

It is immediately evident that one can have a conversion from a life of sin and estrangement to God—this would have been our Lord's first meaning—or from a superficial, rather thoughtless way of supposedly Christian life. The latter is sometimes called a "nominal" Christian life. That is, being a Christian in name but not in action.

We cannot judge anyone but ourselves. Many people may be deeply converted while appearing to lead what we think are rather ordinary lives; and some who are feverishly "religious" may not be deeply committed to Christ at all.

Catholics baptized as babies sometimes grow into the faith so gradually that they never experience any one dramatic moment of conversion. Yet they are indeed wholly "converted" to Christ. On the other hand, it is possible that someone may grow into the external practices of the faith without a deep and personal relationship to Christ.

Each of us must look into his own heart and face reality. Perhaps our whole life has been lived on a superficial level, going through motions. Perhaps—what is more likely—we have been able by the grace of God to enter into the Christian life with sincerity and faithfulness. In one dramatic moment or over a long period of growth, we have come to love God with our whole heart, mind and spirit.

Whole? Each of us must admit that, while our love of God may be basic and fundamental, it is never "whole." There is always an area of our life that we are afraid to give to God. Shall we call this hesitant attitude "sinful"?

At any rate, we must all admit that our conversion is not complete. To say it more bluntly, *the life of a Christian is a life of ongoing, never-ending conversion.* There is indeed a once-and-for-all turning to God whereby we live in God's grace. Yet, we can all say with Saint Francis, "Let us begin to do good, for as yet we have done nothing."

Positive and Negative

Positively, *conversion* and ongoing-conversion means letting the grace of God open us entirely to his will. We become free from every constraint except the *gentle* pressure of God's love. Every day we allow God to open us up, out of our narrowness and rigidity, to the freedom of his own life. Or, more realistically, every day we let God open us up again and again and again.

Negatively, conversion and ongoing conversion are referred to by these words of Christ, "If a man wishes to come after me, he must deny his very self, take up his cross, and begin to follow in my footsteps. Whoever would save his life will lose it, but whoever loses his life for my sake will find it." "Self-denial" here does not mean giving up candy during Lent. It means giving up every claim to our own will, every assertion of independence, every ounce of self-sufficiency. It means taking up the cross of Christ's total and absolute obedience to his Father in life and death.

Self-denial means a once-and-for-all dying and rising with Christ. It means a daily, perhaps hourly, dying to the pressing impulse of selfishness, self-will, doing it "my way," and rising to a conscious and deliberate acceptance of the healing and life-giving power of God.

A Lifelong Vocation

So, penance is nothing but whole Christian life, a joyful-sorrowful rejection of all that cannot advance the glory of God and a peaceful acceptance of God's constant and gentle offer of friendship. Apart from this "conversion penance," all other penance is useless.

Questions for Reflection—What four kinds of penance can you distinguish? What is the two-part definition of penance in general? What is the most important aspect of penance?

Connecting With Scripture and Franciscan Writings—The Mystical Body, the Christian life, the Christian home in Galatians, Chapters 5-6;

Ephesians, Chapters 1-2, 4-6. Bodo, pp. 33-36; Normile, *Following Francis of Assisi*, Chapter 2.

Application to Daily Life—Is penance positive or negative? Do you know of any time or period in your life when you "converted?" How will there always be room for conversion in your life? In daily prayer and at Mass, if possible, pray sincerely for your once-and-ongoing conversion.

Prayer—Sometimes I do your will, Lord, and I thank you for your guidance in those moments. But, there are other times when I resist and break away from you with selfish, willful stubbornness. I am truly sorry for being less than you would have me be. Change me, Lord, change me.... Amen.

From the Rule of the Secular Franciscan Order

7. United by their vocation as "brothers and sisters of penance," and motivated by the dynamic power of the gospel, let them conform their thoughts and deeds to those of Christ by means of that radical interior change which the gospel itself calls "conversion." Human frailty makes it necessary that this conversion be carried out daily.

REFLECTION 13

The Consequences of Penance

"Francis, you must despise and hate all that your body has loved and desired up till now, if you would recognize my will. Once you have begun, you will find that everything which seemed pleasant and sweet to you will turn to unbearable bitterness, but the things that formerly made you shudder will give you peace and joy."

Penance as Self-discipline

After Saint Francis heard the above words from Christ in prayer, he met a leper. Up till then he had regarded such people with great loathing. Now he conquered his revulsion, got down from his horse, gave the leper a coin, and kissed his hand. And the leper gave him the kiss of peace. Then Francis mounted his horse and continued on his way. It was one of the great symbolic acts of his life, leading up to his conversion.

Saint Francis's Rule was comparatively mild in regards to fasting and other penitential practices. At the end of his life he apologized to his "Brother Body" for the harsh penance he had done. But the fact remains that Saint Francis and his friars practiced severe penance, in the second sense described in Reflection 12.

Are Things Any Different Today?

Living in an affluent society, our culture seems to take for granted that pleasure, ease, comfort, softness are almost the be-all and end-all of life. Have we succumbed to a philosophy of hedonism, demanding everything that gratifies the body? Is it true that the only Spartan discipline today is to be found in a professional dancer's studio or a heavyweight boxer's gymnasium?

In the face of all this, it is good to recall the words of Pope Paul VI's Apostolic Constitution on Penance: "The Church urges first of all that everyone practice the virtue of penance by constantly attending to the duties pertaining to his state in life, and by patiently enduring the trials of each day's work here on earth, and the uncertainties of life that cause so much anxiety of mind."

The Church urges all the faithful to live up to the divine commandment of penance by afflicting their bodies by some acts of chastisement, over and above the discomforts and annoyances of everyday life.

"Afflicting their bodies" and "acts of chastisement" sound harsh and foreign to us today. So do the words of Saint Francis: "There are many people who, when they sin or are injured, frequently blame the enemy or their neighbor. But it is not so, because each one has the enemy in his power, that is his body through which he sins. *Blessed is the servant*, then, who always holds captive the enemy delivered into his power and wisely safeguards himself from him; because, as long as he does this, no other enemy visible or invisible will be able to harm him" (Admonition X). Saint Paul puts the matter this way: "I punish my body and enslave it, so that after proclaiming to others I myself should not be disqualified" (1 Corinthians 9:27).

What Are We to Do?

We can scarcely classify Saint Paul, Pope Paul and Saint Francis as anti-body pessimists. They are not Greek idealists, thinking of the body as an unfortunate burden we must carry until our soul is released from its prison. They are all speaking of the impulse that lies in all *persons*, body-spirit beings that we are. No one need ask anyone else about this. We have all experienced the *urge to excess*, the tendency to a mindless and ungoverned grasping and gulping of pleasure, in food or drink or sex or drugs, or in imagination, emotion, anger, or in the pursuit of whatever attracts us.

The practice of self-discipline is not an especially Christian contribution to the life of man. It is the practical common sense even of pagans who realize that if their human faculties are to have their noblest or even most useful expression, they must be moderated, that is, guided by reason.

Christians know the earthly and eternal value of their persons. Their self-denial is not a grim and prideful domineering of their bodies as a matter of personal achievement. Rather it is the commonsense insurance against anything that threatens—and many dangers do threaten—their relationship with Christ.

This penance is, as we have said, saying "no" when we need not so that we can courageously say it when we must. Penance is a practiced "yes" to many good things that might have been left undone in preparation for the many moments when a joyous "yes" is the response God expects.

In Particular

At a time when most in our society are, on the average, fifteen pounds overweight; when organizations like Weight Watchers flourish; when zero-calorie food and drink demonstrate how far we are from under-nourishment, it is certainly time to consider the age-old practice of fasting: abstinence *from food* or *from this food* or *from this much food.* Like the other two elements in the Christian triad of penance—prayer and charity—fasting will never go out of style.

Penance as Atonement

Let us be clear on one point from the beginning: There is no way that a human being can make up for sin by his or her own efforts. Sin begets death in us, total or partial. That which has been killed can only be recreated by God.

We do not go about scraping together our pitiful bits of reparation so that we can bring them to God and purchase forgiveness. We cannot put God in our debt.

The only valid atonement a Christian can contemplate is that of Christ. He alone saves us. He alone makes reparation to the goodness and holiness of God for the offense and damage of sin. He does so by his perfect and childlike love and trust of his Father. In him all the wreck and ruin of human life can be repaired, restored, reconciled to life, "made up for."

Christian atonement is a Christian's letting himself be empowered with the Spirit of Christ in his life and death. His concern is the glory and honor of God, not self-justification, not wiping the slate clean so that God "has nothing on him." Sensing the miracle of God's love, a Christian is appalled and horrified at the malice and brazenness of sin—his own and that of the whole world. He joins his heart and mind to that of Christ's perfect "making up."

Once joined to Christ, a Christian can indeed make atonement, but it must never be thought of as something an individual creates by his own power. We are totally in debt to God whether sinners or just. God is the source of all goodness. We simply accept God's own healing of that which he has created.

Punishment?

What, then, of the terrible sufferings the saints sometimes inflicted on themselves—scourging, for instance? We can only say that if they were saints, they were in total union with Christ. Their penitential practices were merely the tip of the iceberg. They were literally willing to suffer the pains of Christ. They wanted to be plunged into his actual crucifixion. If we ever get that far, we will know what is wise and what is not.

We must never take any accident, suffering, sickness or misfortune as a "punishment" sent from God. If God were in the business of penalties, the job would certainly be done better!

52

Nevertheless, it is healthy for us to recognize the results of sin already contained in the sin. God does not have to "add" punishment to sin—it is already present at the heart of sin itself. There is no greater punishment than to be separated from God. If we sin by hatred, the misery in our heart is the "punishment" of sickness in a precious faculty abused.

Finally, penitential practices allow us to realize the malice of our sin. Without ever losing our self-respect and the wonder of our union with God, we can let ourselves feel the seriousness of our past sins by accepting the sufferings we have or by practicing self-discipline which keeps us from forgetting that we have indeed soiled the very creation of God and by seeking reconciliation.

Summary

Penance, then, is conversion, self-discipline and co-atonement with Christ. It is a lifelong task, never finished. Penance is not a matter of gloom and discouragement, but of hope and confidence and joy tempered by a frank admission of past sins, present and future dangers.

Questions for Reflection—Besides ongoing conversion, what two other aspects of penance are part of the everyday life of a Christian? What does our Christian faith add to the usual practice of asceticism? In what way can we "make reparation" for sin?

Connecting With Scripture and Franciscan Writings—The Christian life, dangers, Christ our head, in Philippians, Chapters 2-3; Colossians, Chapters 1-3. Bodo, pp. 36-39.

Application to Daily Life—What is the area in your life that most needs discipline? What most needs atonement, reparation, reconciliation? You may choose to offer your daily burdens or troubles and some freely chosen self-denial to God in union with Christ.

Prayer—Dear Jesus, I know that fasting is emptying myself so that your Spirit can fill me to overflowing. Reveal to me what I must sacrifice for you—food or drink, lust or gluttony, pride or pleasure-seeking, judgmental nature or critical spirit.... Amen.

REFLECTION 14

The Sacrament of Reconciliation

"I feel that I am the greatest sinner that ever existed."
—*Saint Francis*

A Sign From God

After Jesus made his fundamental demand to "repent and believe the Good News," he gave us a sign whereby we can be certain that God's power is within our repentance and that God's life becomes our new life. This is the Sacrament of Baptism.

A person may turn away from God even after being given this intimate relationship (mortal sinfulness) or to damage that relationship to a degree (venial sinfulness). The Sacrament of Reconciliation is God's way of giving us the sign that he truly reconciles us to himself and to each other.

Social Aspect of Sin

When we destroy or disturb our relationship with God, there is an inevitable effect on our relationship with others and vice versa. We have only one spirit and it affects everything we do, including our relationships with others. Likewise, if there is something sinful about our attitude toward others, this is at the same time an offense against God who has created and loves all of us. The two cannot be separated.

It is also true that if there is something sinful in my attitude, no matter how "secret" I think it is, it has an effect on others. If in no other way, I hurt them by not loving them as they have a right to be loved by Christ's command to me. Sin is never merely a private affair. Every sin is personal but has social ramifications.

Emphasis on these two things focuses the Church's practice of the Sacrament of Reconciliation on our awareness of the social nature of sin, as well as the social nature of forgiveness. When we leave God, we leave his community, the Church. When God reconciles us to himself, he does so through the Church. We are reconciled to that Body which is the visible sign of God's presence in the world, whether we have "left" it totally by mortal sinfulness or partially by lesser sinfulness. Hence, the practice of "communal" penance services with the opportunity for individual reconciliation is an expression of these realities. Sin is my personal responsibility. It affects other people. I can be reconciled to God only if I am reconciled to my neighbor. A communal penance service is a fitting sign that the whole Church welcomes me in forgiveness and that I as a member of the whole Church welcome others in the same way.

Personal Sin

Sin is expressed in external words and actions, especially by omissions. But sin goes much deeper. It brings disorder in our attitudes and value systems. Ultimately, sin affects our "hearts," our inmost self. From there it touches and affects our relationships, our families, our world.

Predominant Fault

Each of us has unique characteristics. If the five people who know us inside out and backwards were asked to describe us in two or three words, they would probably agree in substance: "happy-go-lucky," "perfectionist," "domineering," "quiet/withdrawn," "worrier/analyzer," and so on. Now it should be evident that our sinful attitude is going to be in the "mold" of our predominant characteristic. If Napoleon sins, it's not going to be by pouting or oversensitiveness. It's going to be by running over people with his power. If the life of the party sins, it's going to be by laziness, neglect, lack of self-discipline. If Egghead Egbert sins, it's not going to be by activism or drunkenness but by refusing to help someone in need.

Each of us should try to ferret out our predominant attitude or characteristic—it's evident to anyone who knows us—and see that it is the source of the sinfulness of our lives, no matter how varied its expression.

This is what we bring back, time and again, to the forgiveness of Christ. Again and again we place our weakness within his strength, receive the assurance of his forgiveness and healing and continuing strength.

Reconciliation

When the Church issued its new ritual of the Sacrament of Reconciliation, it seemed to contemplate two things. First, it wanted to create a thorough and serious celebration of the sacrament that reconciles us with our God. This might involve checking our parish schedule of times for Reconciliation or making an appointment with a priest, making serious preparation by prayer, use of Scripture, possibly counseling. Second, it wanted to emphasize the communal celebration of the sacrament, in which the individual confession will be relatively brief, because of the large number of people involved. This confession may be as short as, "My worst sinfulness is an attitude of vindictiveness, and since my last confession I have hurt my husband/wife by a certain coolness, my children by excessive punishment and my friends by mean remarks, ridicule and avoidance."

Ongoing Conversion

Our whole life is ongoing conversion, an attempt to open us up to God more and more. It is also a turning away from sinfulness—the infectious attitudes in us—over and over again. We do this in prayer, in the Eucharist, and in the sacrament that concentrates on our need for reconciliation and the ever-present willingness of God to give it.

Questions for Reflection—Why does all personal sin have social consequences? What is more to be worried about, the act or the attitude? Why? Of what is the Sacrament of Reconciliation a sign?

Connecting With Scripture and Franciscan Writings—The beginning of Holy Week in Mark, Chapters 11-13. Bodo, pp. 39-42.

Application to Daily Life—Do I think of the Sacrament of Reconciliation as a positive celebration of the mercy of God? Is it an act of faith on my part? How can I better determine my characteristic fault? Spend part of your prayer time asking God's forgiveness for your characteristically sinful attitude. Make plans to receive the Sacrament of Reconciliation.

Prayer—I confess, Lord, that I probably know my own unique, predominant fault that leads me to sins of omission and commission but too often I deny that it is present in me. Make me honest with myself and with you so that I can offer this fault for your healing. Amen.

From the Rule of the Secular Franciscan Order
Concerning Those Who Do Not Do Penance (Prologue)

But all those men and women who are not doing penance and do not receive the Body and Blood of our Lord Jesus Christ and live in vices and sin and yield to evil concupiscence and to the wicked desires of the flesh, and do not observe what they have promised to the Lord, and are slaves to the world in their bodies, by carnal desires and the anxieties and cares of this life (cf. John 8:41).

These are blind, because they do not see the true light, our Lord Jesus Christ; they do not have spiritual wisdom because they do not have the Son of God who is the true wisdom of the Father. Concerning them, it is said "Their skill was swallowed up" (Psalm 107:27) and "you rebuke the cursed proud who turn away from your commands" (Psalm 119:21). They see and acknowledge, they know and do bad things and knowingly destroy their own souls.

See, you who are blind, deceived by your enemies, the world, the flesh and the devil, for it is pleasant to the body to commit sin and it is bitter to make it serve God because all vices and sins come out and "proceed from the heart of man" as the Lord says in the gospel (cf. Matthew 7:21). And you have nothing in this world and in the next, and you thought you would possess the vanities of this world for a long time.

But you have been deceived, for the day and the hour will come to which you give no thought and which you do not know and of which you are ignorant. The body grows infirm, death approaches, and so it dies a bitter death, and no matter where or when or how man dies, in the guilt of sin, without penance or satisfaction, though he can make satisfaction but does not do it.

The devil snatches the soul from his body with such anguish and tribulation that no one can know it except he who endures it, and all the talents and power and "knowledge and wisdom" (2 Chronicles 1:17) which they thought they had will be taken away from them (cf. Luke 8:18; Mark 4:25), and they leave their goods to relatives and friends who take and divide them and say afterwards, "Cursed be his soul because he could have given us more, he could have acquired more than he did." The worms eat up the body and so they have lost body and soul during this short earthly life and will go into the inferno where they will suffer torture without end.

All those into whose hands this letter shall have come we ask in the charity that is God (cf. 1 John 4:17) to accept kindly and with divine love the fragrant words of our Lord Jesus Christ quoted above. And let those who do not know how to read have them read to them.

And may they keep them in their mind and carry them out, in a holy manner to the end, because they are "spirit and life" (John 6:64).

And those who will not do this will have to render "an account on the day of judgment" (cf. Matthew 12:36) before the tribunal of our Lord Jesus Christ (cf. Romans 14:10).

REFLECTION 15

The Poverty of Christ

"I, Brother Francis, wish to follow after the life and poverty of our highest Lord, Jesus Christ, and of his most holy mother, and I will hold out in this to the last."

—Saint Francis

Why Was Jesus Poor?

First and before all, Francis wanted simply to imitate the poverty of Christ. He was no idealist pursuing an abstract ideal. He saw the clear picture of the Gospels—a Christ who had nowhere to lay his head, and Francis responded, "Whatever he did, I want to do." This fundamental lesson of Franciscan poverty must never be forgotten. Poverty, in the sense of non-possession, is neither good nor bad—it is simply a fact. What makes gospel poverty valuable is its purpose: the imitation of Christ *for the purpose* of Christ. Saint Paul's great hymn speaks of Jesus' "emptying" himself, foregoing the glory to which he had a right as God, entering into human nature in all its limitation, weakness and suffering (Philippians 2:6-11). Jesus went as far as he could. Obviously he could not take upon himself sin or the immediate results of sin, bad habits, concupiscence. But he took all the sad as well as glorious inheritance of human nature all the way to that point. Why?

By entering into the weakness and damages that sin had caused to us, Jesus could heal it by the holiness of his inner spirit. No matter what suffering he underwent, what frustration, misunderstanding, injustice, pain, deprivation or poverty he endured, his human spirit was always directed in simple trust to the Father's praise. Francis had an intuition of the beauty of Christ's poverty. He wrote no profound philosophical analysis of this. He simply imitated it.

Jesus, the Trusting Son

In Jesus we realize that nothing can remain purely negative. What was the result of his entering into human poverty with a totally loving trust? He was able to enjoy all the things of earth that happened to

59

come his way. He saw all creation as praising God, not as something to be grabbed, hidden or sold. He saw all God's gifts as the inheritance of all people, to be shared in justice and charity. He saw all creation as the possession of everyone.

Blessed Are You Poor

Jesus was the final flower of a movement that began in the Old Testament. At first the poor were merely the miserable victims of society's greed and cruelty. As time went on, it came to be realized that since they were the victims of injustice, God had to be on their side. Their only trust was in God for the practical reason that there was no one else to go to. Gradually the "poor" became those who were totally dependent on God. They were the *anawim* to whom God said, "Blessed are you poor." They did not put their trust in earthly things, whether they possessed them or not. The poorest of all these *anawim* of the Old Testament was the virgin of Nazareth. Because she was completely free of all selfish attachments, completely open to God, Mary was the perfect virginal dwelling place in which the Word could "empty" himself into *her* kind of spiritual poverty as well as the material poverty of his brothers and sisters.

This was the vision of Francis, and this was certainly the reason why he always joined Jesus and his mother in his praise of poverty.

The Question Remains

We have still not settled the "practical" question as to whether poverty is material or spiritual, whether it is mainly positive or negative, whether it is mainly an ascetical practice or a generous sharing of this world's goods with others. It is possible for a materially wealthy person to be totally unattached to her possessions. And a very poor person in terms of possessions can be stingy, grasping and hoarding. If we place the question within the mystery of Christ, perhaps we can see that there is no neat answer that can be printed in a catechism.

Lady Poverty

Typically, Francis made poverty the lady he served as a knight of Christ. It was a true romance—a far-off ideal, almost impossible. Yet, a hard reality lived in the cold of Rivo Torto, the nausea of begged food that came close to being garbage, and in the desolation of being laid naked on the ground as he approached death in imitation of his master. Only Lady Poverty, he said, could follow Christ even up on the cross in total deprivation and nakedness before God.

Questions for Reflection—Why did Christ become human as we are?

What is the central important reality about the poverty of Christ? Who are the *anawim* today?

Connecting With Scripture and Franciscan Writings—The last judgment in Matthew, Chapters 24-25; Luke, Chapter 21. Bodo, pp. 42-45; Normile, *Following Francis of Assisi*, Chapter 4.

Application to Daily Life—How does the spirit of gospel poverty apply to buying a car, a home, entertainment? How does it enter into the raising of children? Is it possible to be "gospel poor" in our affluent society? Take some material possession—clothing, food, a car—and see it not as a possession but as an instrument for serving God. Deliberately share some valuable possession with another person.

Prayer—Lord, show me how to be poor in a culture that worships the wealth of power, possessions and prestige. Amen.

From the Rule of the Secular Franciscan Order

11. Trusting in the Father, Christ chose for himself and his mother a poor and humble life, even though he valued created things attentively and lovingly. Let the Secular Franciscans seek a proper spirit of detachment from temporal goods by simplifying their own material needs. Let them be mindful that according to the gospel they are stewards of the goods received for the benefit of God's children.

    Thus, in the spirit of "the Beatitudes," and as pilgrims and strangers on their way to the home of the Father, they should strive to purify their hearts from every tendency and yearning for possession and power.

REFLECTION 16

Poverty for the Kingdom

"Once, when he (Saint Francis) was returning from Siena, he met a beggar and said to his companion, 'We must give back to the poor little man the cape that belongs to him, for we have only received it as a loan until we meet someone who is poorer than we.'"

—*The Writings of Brother Leo*

Why "Poverty?"

Poverty, both rightly and wrongly understood, has been the badge of Saint Francis and of his Order from the beginning. He is known as the "poor little man of Assisi." His first Rule was largely a collection of Scripture texts on poverty. The crises in the Order, even during the life of Saint Francis, have hinged on the interpretation of Gospel poverty. The ideal and practice of poverty are still the challenging, perplexing problem of Franciscans today.

The problem has three parts: 1) What kind of poverty is Jesus talking about? Luke's Gospel says, "Blessed are you poor." Matthew's Gospel says "Blessed are the poor in spirit." Are we called to material or "spiritual" poverty? Can they be separated? 2) Is poverty primarily a not-having, a form of asceticism and purification, or does it have a more important and positive orientation? 3) Is poverty an inward-looking virtue, something primarily concerned with the holiness of those who practice it, or is its real purpose the sharing of earthly goods with others? We will try to consider these problems in this and the following chapters. Then we will discuss the "sister" of poverty—humility.

The Love of Money Is the Root of All Evil

Whatever else gospel poverty is, it is an attack on the root of all evil, greed. Money is neither good nor bad in itself. Money can buy medicine for a friend or poison for an enemy. Not having money can produce saints or criminals. The virtue of gospel poverty frees us from an unreasonable or slavish attachment to things. The Holy Spirit has told us that the *love* of money is the root of all evil (1 Timothy 6:10). Therefore, in the logic of Saint Bonaventure, detachment from an unreasonable love of money must be the root of all good. It is the enslavement to money that is evil. Money can buy pleasure, prestige, power. These can become insatiable—the more I get, the more I want. So, for all Christians, the virtue of gospel poverty is necessary to curb and control this basic danger in our weakened human nature, the tendency to bow down before Mammon.

Material or Spiritual?

The *Jerome Biblical Commentary* has this to say: "The difference between Luke's 'poor' and Matthew's 'poor in spirit' is not substantial. Matthew certainly does not mean those who, although they are wealthy, are spiritually detached from their wealth.... Both phrases designate the poor class, which constituted the vast majority of the population.... Matthew's 'poor in spirit' emphasizes less the literal lack of possessions than the lowly condition of the poor; their poverty did not allow them the arrogance and assertiveness of the wealthy but imposed habitual and servile deference. The term is very close to 'meek' in the third beatitude" (*Jerome Biblical Commentary*, 43:30).

At a discussion of religious poverty, one participant made a telling remark, "Look, to be poor means not to have access to *power*. As long as we have power, let's not say we are practicing 'poverty!'" Gospel poverty, it would seem, must have some effect on the material things we have and use. At the very least, it calls for a *sparing* use of things, both as ascetical practice and as a means of sharing our goods with others.

The problem will not be solved by a blueprint of observances. Rather, the answer can only come from a more basic question: How will someone act in regard to his money and possessions once the love of Christ has possessed his heart, and he sees the whole world as God's gift and sees all men and women as his brothers and sisters and the whole world as God's gift to all his children?

Poverty Makes Us Free

But let us never forget the purpose of the virtue which is freedom to love God. The Bible speaks of "the freedom of the children of God," and Christ said, "If you continue in my word, you are truly my disciples; and you will know the truth, and the truth will make you free" (John 8:32). Freedom negatively means the absence of slavery to sin, death and the devil. Positively put, freedom means the power to be like God by our choice. The danger to mankind is that it becomes enslaved by the physical pleasures of the body and the selfish pleasures of pride and self-love. Poverty is designed to make us free of any enslavement to things and also to persons, places, circumstances and desires. Saint Francis saw the danger of being attached to anyone or anything to the degree that perfect love of God would become difficult or even impossible. He wanted to be in no danger of preferring anything else to God.

Poverty for Others

The social and economic situation in the world today makes it impossible to divorce any discussion of gospel poverty from a Christian concern for justice to the poor and deprived—both individuals and nations. As the quotation at the beginning of this chapter indicates, Saint Francis felt that anything he had or used was a generous loan from God, to be held in stewardship until someone poorer than he came along. He was always giving away his cloak to beggars. He gave away the only copy of the New Testament the friars had so that a poor woman could buy bread.

A modern spiritual writer has suggested that the vow of poverty be renamed. He suggested "generous sharing" instead. Indeed, such an emphasis will save the practice of poverty from being a sterile, self-conscious and introverted practice that does no more than flatter the pride of the practitioner. Charity to others for the love of God is the primary virtue. To be poor before God is to be totally open to his gifts and then totally open to the needs of others—for whose sake the gifts are given to us.

Therefore, each member of the Secular Franciscan Order must ask: "What can I do every day, within the actual circumstances and obligations of my life, to cut any creeping enslavement to money or possessions? What will make me free? What needs of others can I fulfill with my monetary support or outright gift?" Like Saint Francis, we have no rules for this. As he said, "The Lord showed me what to do."

Questions for Reflection—Negatively, from what does the spirit of poverty free us? Positively, what does the spirit of poverty produce in us? What is poverty?

Scripture Reading for the Week—Words of our Lord at the Last Supper and the beginning of the passion in John, Chapters 15-17. Bodo, pp. 45-47.

Application to Daily Life—What evidences of slavish attachment to things, arrangements, comforts can you find in your life? How can a rich man be poor in spirit? How can a poor man be greedy? How can I develop real freedom through poverty in my life? Try to discover evidence of greed in your life. Deny yourself something and give it to God through others.

Prayer—"Thy kingdom come, thy will be done"—with my time, my possessions, my talents, my bank account, my wages, my love, my.... Amen.

From the Rule of the Secular Franciscan Order

10. Uniting themselves to the redemptive obedience of Jesus, who placed his will into the Father's hands, let them faithfully fulfill the duties proper to their various circumstances of life. Let them also follow the poor and crucified Christ, witnessing to him even in difficulties and persecutions.

Some External Applications of Poverty

"[S]omeone who is truly poor in spirit hates himself and loves those who strike him on the cheek."

—*Saint Francis*, Admonition XIV

Franciscan Poverty as a Spirit and a Practice

The "spirit of poverty" is the attitude of being free, not enslaved by money and what money can buy. We are not discontented with the limitations that our lack of money imposes upon us. We try to live our lives with the things we really need, instead of letting our desires control our life. Franciscan poverty flees from luxury and loves the things that give less pleasure to the ego and to vanity.

It Flees Luxury

Perhaps we will be helped here by a dictionary definition of luxury: "A free indulgence in costly food, dress or anything which gratifies the appetites or tastes; also a mode of life characterized by such material abundance." It is a *free indulgence*. Here "free" means "with no restraint." Fallen human nature hates restraint. It thinks that happiness consists in "freely" doing whatever pleases passion or pride. But Christ says we are free if we love God and are not the slaves of sin. In other words, if we deny ourselves and say "yes!" to God, we are free. We are free from all harm and free to accept the happiness God offers us.

Less, Rather Than More

Poverty loves things that give less pleasure to the ego and to vanity. Notice, first, it loves. That is, it sees good in ordinary things. We are not told to "put up with" or "grimly suffer" things that give less pleasure. We are to be cheerful, glad, and perfectly willing not to have the latest car, the fanciest clothing or the most expensive house. There is nothing wrong with what pleases the eye: flowers, faces, a clean, well-kept house. The danger is in the vanity, the conceit, the greed that often lurks beneath. So, Secular Franciscans will try to give their children reasonable advancement in things worthwhile—art or science, craftsmanship or culture. They may relieve the burdens of home maintenance by acquiring work-savers. They may save for a home in the country where their children will have more fresh air. However, they refuse to be slaves to pleasure, prestige or power.

Avoiding Extremes

Secular Franciscans avoid extremes of cost and style, observing the golden mean suited to each one's station in life. A bank president would hardly be expected to come to work on a bicycle. A college student would be foolish not to buy the books needed because of a mistaken idea of practicing poverty. A mother would not be reasonable in refusing a birthday party to her children because of a "spirit" of poverty. But the bank president, the college student and the mother each have a hundred chances a day to break the "accumulative" habit that wants to dominate their lives, enslaving them to things instead of making things serve them.

Secular Franciscans avoid vanity in their appearance and clothes and adhere to the standard of simplicity, moderation and propriety that benefits each one. With regard to food and drink, they observe the frugality recommended by the Rule.

Spending Money

Our society is characterized by impulse-buying and consumerism. Perhaps never in history have people indulged in such wasteful buying of luxuries, duplicates, gadgets. Credit-card debt plagues multitudes. But gospel poverty is not mere thrift. Still less is it miserliness. Gospel poverty is simply a clear decision to use God's gifts with reason. Gospel poverty refuses to keep up with the Joneses. It does not try to maintain a posture at any cost. Gospel poverty it does not deny self or children necessary or reasonable things in order to buy "prestige" things.

Teaching Young People Responsibility

Neither children nor their parents may overlook the former's responsibility to the family bank account. The earning of money does not give youngsters a right to spend it as they please. They should realize the need to pay for some of their clothes, to save for their future education and insurance, perhaps to pay for some of the food and other necessities of the family depending on the family's circumstances. Not all of their money should go to the basic items unless the family is in dire need. Young people should cooperate with their parents in estimating how much will be spent for recreation, how much will be saved, how much will be given as a fair share of family expenses.

The Broad View

In the Synod of 1971, the representative bishops of the world together with the Holy Father to issue a now famous document. Its recommendations include the following: (Francis, as a loyal son of the Church, would have observed them faithfully.)

> *As regards temporal possessions, it must never happen that the Gospel witness which the Church is required to give become ambiguous. The preservation of certain positions of privilege must constantly be submitted to this principle.*

> *Although it is difficult, in general, to draw a line between what is needed for right use and what is demanded by prophetic witness, we must certainly keep firmly to this principle: Our faith demands of us a certain sparingness of use, and the Church is obliged to live and administer its own goods in such a way that the Gospel is proclaimed to the poor.*

> *Our examination of conscience now comes to the life-style of all: bishops, priests, religious and lay people.... In societies enjoying a higher level of consumer spending, it must be asked whether our life-style exemplifies that sparingness with regard to consumption which we preach to others as necessary that so many millions of hungry people in the world may be fed....*

> *The radical transformation of the world in the Paschal Mystery of the Lord gives full meaning to the efforts of men, in particular the young, to lessen injustice, freedom, brotherhood and love.*

Questions for Reflection—What defines luxury? Is a birthday party according to gospel poverty? A new car? Always? Explain.

Connecting With Scripture and Franciscan Writings—The passion and death of Christ in Matthew, Chapters 26-27. Bodo, pp. 47-49.

Application to Daily Life—What impulse buying have you done lately? What can you give up in order to make a donation to a needy family or cause? What does turning the other cheek have to do with poverty? Try to practice "a certain sparingness" in food and drink and to give what you save to a charitable cause.

Prayer—Free me, Lord, from the bondage of too much. Unclutter my life from the tyranny of "things." Lead me on the path of simple living. Amen.

Humility, the Twin of Poverty

*"A man is what he is in the sight of God, and nothing more. If the
Lord should take from me his treasure, which he has loaned me, what
else would remain to me except a body and soul, no different from
that of the infidels?"*

—Saint Francis

Humility and Poverty

Saint Francis, in his simple wisdom, saw poverty and humility as twins.
We are absolutely dependent on God for all things: That is humility.
And God will provide them: That is poverty. We are nothing without
God: That is humility. We want nothing but God: That is poverty. As
creatures, we are poor before God: That is both poverty and humility.
Humility is a virtue whereby we realize and act according to our noth-
ingness apart from God and our complete dependence upon God.

Humility, Foundation of Virtue

Christ began his Sermon on the Mount with the Beatitudes. He began the
Beatitudes with "Blessed are the poor in spirit" (Matthew 5:3). This has
two meanings: 1) How happy are they who are free because of their spirit
of Gospel poverty. 2) How happy are they who realize and admit that
they are absolutely poor before God and thus see everything as a gift.

The fundamental statement of the negative and positive aspect of
humility was made by our Lord. "Those who abide in me and I in them
bear much fruit, because apart from me you can do nothing" (John 15:5).

Nothingness and Dependence

Nothing can exist without God. Our hearts will not beat another beat,
our next breath will not be drawn unless God keeps on maintaining our
lives. We cannot raise a finger a fraction of an inch or love our neighbor
unless God keeps us alive. Humility is, therefore, a deep and simple
virtue. It acknowledges our absolute nothingness without God, and our
complete and absolute dependence on God every second of every day.

"Not that we are competent of ourselves to claim anything as coming from us; our competence is from God" (2 Corinthians 3:5). It is very hard for proud human beings to believe this basic truth of all life.

The Humility of Christ

Humility in this sense was in Christ. His human nature was as dependent on the divine as we are. Therefore, Jesus had to say: "'...I do nothing on my own, but I speak these things as the Father instructed me. And the one who sent me is with me; he has not left me alone, for I always do what is pleasing to him'" (John 8:28). Mary, in all her immaculate beauty of soul, had to say, "Here am I, the servant of the Lord; let it be with me according to your word" (Luke 1:38). She was nothing without God. How much more we who have added the insult of sin to the fact of nothingness ought to recognize this Christ as our model in humility. Just as he depended on his Father, so we must depend on God.

Are We Worthless?

One of the greatest tragedies of life is the self-hate or the lack of a sense of self-worth that afflicts many people—sometimes without their realizing it. They feel completely insecure. How can anyone love them since they are not worth loving? How can they love others since they have nothing to give? How can they believe that others really love them since they are nothing?

This attitude does not reflect humility but emotional sickness, the terrible result of others' lack of love. Anyone who is truly humble before God has heard the Good News, that God has made us really "something"—his children. And God loves us!

What Is Pride?

Pride, humility's opposite, is the infected heart of all sin. It says, "I am somebody, all by myself. I am independent, worthwhile, all by myself. I need no one, not even God." Another type of pride says, "Well, I need God for the big and unusual things, but I can handle the ordinary things myself. So, I'll pray in time of war, sickness, storms, but I don't really need God's help to breathe, eat or be honest."

Or it says, "My talents are mine. I will show them off and take the credit. My ideas are important. My preferences must be respected. My ideas are not to be questioned." The tragedy of so many good people is the infection of pride that runs through their whole lives. One can be proud of the holiest things such as prayer and kindness. One can even be proud of humility!

The Humility of Saint Francis

Saint Francis always mentioned humility in the same breath with poverty. In a sense, they are the same—personal "without-ness." This is a fact, because all that we have is from God. This is an ideal, because we want to be without everything but God. Some of the most striking things Saint Francis said concern humility: "A man is what he is in the sight of God and nothing more;" "The better a man really is, the worse he feels himself to be." The more we appreciate God's gifts and unending generosity, the more we become conscious of: 1) Our refusing to admit this; 2) Our spoiling of God's precious gifts. As with Saint Paul, the only thing Francis would take "pride" in was the "cross of Christ."

"Worthless Slaves"

Even while he was the happiest of men, Francis still felt himself to be the worst sinner in the world. No one ever took more seriously Christ's words, "When you have done all you have been commanded, say, 'We are worthless slaves; we have done only what we ought to have done'" (Luke 17:10). The follower of Christ was trying to keep a perfect balance: realizing his nothingness but believing in God's love.

> In a picture of our Lord or the Blessed Virgin painted on wood, our Lord and the Blessed Virgin are honored, and yet the wood and the painting ascribe nothing of it to themselves. So the servant of God is a kind of painting of God in which God is honored. But the servant ought to attribute nothing to himself. In comparison with God he is even less than wood or painting. Indeed he is pure nothing.
> (Saint Francis)

Questions for Reflection—What is humility? What words best describe the ingredients of humility? What is the worst sin of all?

Connecting With Scripture and Franciscan Writings—The Resurrection and Ascension in Matthew, Chapter 28; Luke, Chapter 24; John, Chapters 20-21; Acts, Chapter 1. Bodo, pp. 49-51.

Application to Daily Life—What things do you like to think you can do without God's help? Which saying of Saint Francis on humility strikes you most forcibly? Try deliberately to credit God with the talents you have and the good you do. Take responsibility for the evil you find in yourself.

Prayer—"Of myself I can do nothing." I praise you and thank you, my Creator, for what you choose to do in and through me. Amen.

Humility Toward Others

*"I admonish and exhort them (the friars) not to despise or judge peo-
ple they see dressed in soft and showy garments and using choice food
or drink, but rather let each one judge and despise himself."*
—Saint Francis

God's Gifts

If we are humble before God, we cannot be conceited before others.
Humility recognizes the great truth: Everything is from God. If everything is God's, what point is there in comparison? Is God jealous of
himself? He gives this man or woman this or that talent, money, honor,
status. He has given me perhaps more, perhaps less. What's the difference? It's all God's! Shall I be unhappy because God has given a gift to
another "Is thy eye evil because I am good?" To Francis, living the
gospel life meant charity, not judging others. He was not worried about
measuring his gifts against those of others. He simply wanted to give
everybody as much of God's treasure as possible. If God gives us a gift
which he did not give to another, he did it for just one reason: that we
produce fruit with it. We are not better or worse than others. We are
simply what God made us. A pencil is neither better nor worse than a
cup or candle. Each has its own work to do.

Judging Others

In plain truth, we can't judge others. We ourselves certainly do not wish
to be judged by externals. They never express what we are deep down.
What do we know, then, of what others are like on the inside? Someone
seems to be bad. What do we know of his past experiences, parents,
home life, education, temptations, emotions, the bad influences he has
suffered, the cruelty or deception inflicted on him, the ignorance, pain,
physical or mental sickness, worry, misunderstanding that have entered
his life? Who but God knows the human heart? Even when someone
seems to be certainly evil—deliberately so, bragging of it—we still have
the principle of Saint Bonaventure: "I must consider myself below oth-

ers, not because I am certain that I am, but because I am more certain of my unworthiness than I am of theirs." We can appreciate only our own toothache—and our own sin.

Saint Francis: A Humble Man

Brother Masseo once said to Francis:

> I wonder why the whole world runs after you! You are not handsome; you are not deeply learned; you are not of noble birth!" Francis said, "Do you wish to know? I know the answer from the all-seeing God, whose eyes see the good and the bad all over the earth. For those most holy eyes have nowhere seen a greater, more miserable, poorer sinner than I; because in all the earth he has found no more wretched being to do his wonderful work. Therefore, he has chosen me, so as to put to shame the noble and the great, that all may know that all power and virtue come from him, and not from creatures, and no one can exalt himself before his face (Little Flowers).

Saint Francis turned out to be a great reformer although he did not start out to reform. That is, he did not start out condemning those who disagreed with him. He simply worked by prayers and penance to give everybody their inheritance from God. He had such far-reaching influence because no one is afraid of a humble man.

Judging Myself

Saint Francis had a horror of seeming better than he was. He told his friars, after an act of charity, that he was tempted to be vain. On Easter Sunday he got up before the people and made known that he had eaten chicken during Lent (as the doctor had ordered him). When his health required wearing warmer clothing, a fox-pelt over his stomach, he insisted that one be sewn on the outside also so that everyone would see how "self-indulgent" he was. At night he would pretend to sleep and later rise when he thought no one was watching to spend long hours in prayer.

Lesser Brothers

Humility was in the very name he gave his friars: the Friars Minor or "lesser brothers." The minors of his day were the same as they are now—the little people, noble only in their goodness, not particularly distinguished in the eyes of the world. A Secular Franciscan today must continue this spirit. He or she may be high in the world of business, art or science and may be endowed with great talents of mind, body or grace, but in the spirit of Saint Francis, the Secular Franciscan must fight against the infection of pride and the alluring temptation to act only to impress others and draw their flattery. He must remember that he is very little—in fact, nothing of himself. She must constantly recognize the sin within all sins: pride. Summary: These, then, are some principles of humility:

- Our bodies and souls, the grace of God within us, all goodness, virtue, holiness are gifts of God.

- Your talents, money, car, job, family, friends, vocation, home, all are gifts of God.

- You are free to love or ignore God, but even your freedom is God's continuing gift.

- You cannot judge others. You dare not judge others. You can only wish them goodness. You know your own sin; you're not sure of theirs.

- Mental health, peace and happiness depend on the truth of God which is humility.

- Humility is truth. It is not wrong to admit that you have talent or ability but it is very wrong if you feel these belong to you. They are God's.

Questions for Reflection—What is the only answer to the temptation to compare yourself with others? Why are you unable to judge others' guilt? What did Saint Bonaventure say about others who seem to be worse than you are? Who are "minors" in the Franciscan sense?

Connecting With Scripture and Franciscan Writings—Pentecost in Acts, Chapters 2-4. Bodo, pp. 51-54.

Application to Daily Life—If you have twice as much talent from God (in homemaking, computer skills, music, art, labor skills) as another, what does God expect? In what area of God's gifts do you tend to think you are better than others (by your own efforts, of course)? Humble people don't try to "prove" anything. Witnessing the external circumstances of crime, sin and human weakness, try to say with Saint Francis, "There, but for the grace of God, go I! That's me, in different disguise!"

Prayer—I will try to remember, Lord, that your Spirit lives in each person I meet—the proud and the downtrodden, the beautiful and the homely, the wise and the ignorant, the good and the not-so-good. Keep me mindful that at times I may be like each of them. Amen.

From the Rule of the Secular Franciscan Order

13. As the Father sees in every person the features of his Son, the firstborn of many brothers and sisters, so the Secular Franciscans, with a gentle and courteous spirit, accept all people as a gift of the Lord and an image of Christ.

    A sense of community will make them joyful and ready to place themselves on an equal basis with all people, especially with the lowly for whom they shall strive to create conditions of life worthy of people redeemed by Christ.

A Life of Chastity

"It was impossible to say anything really bad about Francis. In all that related to the other sex he was a model. It was known among his friends that no one dare say an evil word in his hearing. If it happened, at once his face assumed a serious, almost harsh, expression, and he did not answer. Like all the pure of heart, Francis had great reverence for the mysteries of life."

—*Jorgensen,* The Life of St. Francis

Parallel with the "sexual revolution" that has discarded most Christian sexual values, there has been a healthy swing from a negative to a positive emphasis in Catholic moral theology. It begins with the fact that all human persons are sexual. Tom thinks, feels, acts as a male human person. Helen lives and loves as a female human person. Sexuality is an inseparable element of human life. It cannot be considered by itself apart from persons in relationships that are loving. In other words, as God made us, sexuality is coextensive with human life. It should not be considered primarily or solely in terms of intercourse (genital sexuality) or marriage. These are not the only manifestations of sexuality. Some people may never marry, never procreate, yet they remain as fully sexual as those who do. They live in loving relationships as this particular man or this individual woman.

The Virtue of Chastity

Chastity is the virtue (habit, attitude, ongoing practice) which reverences and orders sexuality according to God's will. In marriage, it integrates the full use and enjoyment of sexual powers with the unselfish and reverential relationship of love between husband and wife. In the single life, it moderates and guides a man or woman's life as sexual while abstaining from genital sexuality. In either case, it is respect, born of faith, for all persons as temples of the Holy Spirit.

The positive emphasis on the healthiness and holiness of sexuality may be said to have started on the first page of the Bible. "Male and female he created them...and God saw that it was good." The obvious meaning of sexuality is that all human beings need each other.

What is more, God himself was "made flesh," had sexuality. If we didn't catch the goodness from the fact of creation, we certainly can't miss it from the fact that Jesus was a fully sexual human male—something for all believers in the Incarnation to ponder.

The Negative Aspect

All this is not to deny that chastity also looks to the ever-present dangers to chastity and concerns itself with the impulses of human nature that are always tending to be excessive. But even these cannot be separated from the overall moral dangers—summed up in selfishness. Sin, as well as virtue, involves the whole person.

The spirit of chastity, like that of poverty, is a quest for and a preservation of freedom. Those whose sexuality is aligned with God's will are truly free. They use God's gift according to the relationships into which he has put them. They do not let themselves be enslaved to anyone or anything but God.

Chastity of the Married

Husbands and wives fulfill one of the purposes of marriage—mutual love—in a particularly blessed way. They love each other like Christ and the Church. They can no more be separated or be unfaithful than Christ and the Church can.

> *Be subject to one another out of reverence for Christ....*
>
> *Husbands, love your wives, just as Christ loved the church and gave himself up for her, in order to make her holy by cleansing her with the washing of water by the word, so as to present the church to himself in splendor...so that she may be holy and without blemish....*
> *[H]usbands should loves their wives as they do their own bodies. He who loves his wife loves himself.... This is a great mystery, and I am applying it to Christ and the church. Each of you, however, should love his wife as himself, and a wife should respect her husband (Ephesians 5:21-33).*

The Single

Those whom God has given the single vocation are called to let their sexuality be a sign of God's love in a way different from that of married people. The love in marriage is a sign of how particularly God loves each one of us. The chastity of single life is also a sign of God's love and openness to all.

Widows

Saint Paul has this to say about the good qualities to be looked for in widows, especially those who were to be enrolled in a kind of confraternity devoted to Christian chastity:

> "Honor widows who are really widows.... The real widow, left alone, has set her hope on God and continues in supplications and prayers night and day...she must be well attested for her good works, as one who has brought up children, shown hospitality, washed the saints' feet, helped the afflicted, and devoted herself to doing good in every way" (1 Timothy 5:3-10).

Questions for Reflection—Does one pray as a woman, or as a man, or as "generally human?" What is chastity? Why did God make us sexual?

Connecting With Scripture and Franciscan Writings—Saul becomes Paul in Acts, Chapters 8, 9, 22 and 26. Bodo, pp. 54-56.

Application to Daily Life—If you are a married person, how can you increase your respect for your partner and thus ensure the full and God-given enjoyment of marriage? If you are single, what masculine or feminine qualities make you a sign of God's love and openness to all? In prayer, meditate on the wholeness and healthiness of your personality as God wants it to be. Ask for increased commitment to others in the various relationships of your life.

Prayer—Lord, show me how chastity means reserving the best of myself for you while sharing the best of you with others. Amen.

Youth—Hope for the Future

"You are the hope of the Church and of the world. You are my hope"
—*Pope John Paul II to the youth of the world, quoted in* Crossing
the Threshold of Hope

Youth are the hope of our families, our country, our Church and our world. Because of that honored place that young people hold, Secular Franciscans are renewing efforts to provide a place for youth to learn of the Franciscan-Christian way of life. Youth groups are scattered throughout the country. (For information on groups in your area, call 1-800-FRANCIS.)

Vatican II called all Catholics to work for a good world, to see the world as God's creation, sometimes distorted and abused, but always holy and deserving respect. We are called to make this world as good a living place as possible for young and not-so-young alike.

Whether we like it or not, the world is upon us like a flood. Electronics and technology unimaginable a decade ago are probably the best symbols of what has happened. Almost without thinking, we see events around the world. We communicate with people everywhere instantaneously.

Partly by vocation, then, and partly by the nature of things, we are immersed in a good-bad world. And we have gotten used to a lot of things. Or have we? Older people today are, or used to be, surprised, worried or shocked at the results of the sexual revolution—cohabitation; college, high school and even grade school students engaging in sex as recreation; pornography; gay activism; near-nudity in some fashion styles, rampant materialism. How can a Christian, especially a young one, be "in" this world and not be "of" it?

What Christ Calls For

We do get used to things and today there is a happy absence of an unhealthy preoccupation with the slightest dangers of sexual sin which once was fairly common. But where are the limits? What are the ideals of chastity that never change?

We don't start with a list of actions that are wrong but with one attitude that is right: Every human being is sacred to God, purchased by the blood of Christ, hovered over by the Spirit. The *whole* person, inseparably body and spirit, is sacred. I may not use or abuse any person's mind, talents, emotions or body for my selfish purposes. Whether for sexual, materialistic or intellectual gratification, I may never see another person as a "thing."

Only this deep Christian love for others can withstand the call to the enjoyment of every possible pleasure today. Blatant and expertly rationalized arguments pour over us twenty-four hours a day. "You have a right to be free." "Do your own thing." "It's my money. I earned it so I can spend it however I please." "It's nobody else's business." "We're not hurting anybody." "We love each other." "We're consenting adults," "It's *just* a movie. What's wrong with seeing it?" The list goes on.

A Christian believes the act of sexual intercourse is reserved by God's law for those who have committed themselves to each other for life in a loving marriage. Since this is so, a reasonable and prayerful effort must be made to control the attitudes, expressions of affection, emotional involvement, the visual stimulations of videos and movies and even music, which can sometimes irresistibly glamorize sexual intercourse. Styles change, knowledge and maturity grow, but human nature remains the same. We have not grown up beyond a point where the normal dangers of touch, fantasy, reading, entertainment and dating are slight ones. If this were so, a large part of our advertising would have disappeared long ago.

Responsibility

But, again, a list of "occasions of sin" is not our first need. What we need first is a deep sense of responsibility—response-ability. You may be a high school senior or a business major in college. You are part of a group of people who are called individually and as a community to be the Body of Christ. You have the power to answer that call courageously and faithfully. You have the holiness and power of Christ's own spirit within you. You can answer the call to "glorify God and bear him in your bodies." You can be a powerful witness in the worst of circumstances to the presence of Christ. Your unselfishness, respect for others, desire for material things, the good works you do to make others' lives better, your reverence for your own body and theirs as part of your whole Christian commitment to Christ speak to every person you meet. They may not admit it. They may ridicule it in embarrassment. They may react in anger but they cannot fail to get the message.

Preparation for a Life Commitment

Most young people are called to the sacrament of marriage. They are preparing and being prepared for this from the moment they are born by experiencing the love of good parents, learning unselfishness, respect, concern and responsibility.

Before marriage or adult single life can be successful, individuals must learn to live for others, not just themselves. They can find joy in using the creativity and energy of youth in athletic endeavors, music, art, work projects in poor areas of their city, visiting the lonely elderly in nursing homes. Such activities create wholesome life-styles. Self-esteem grows as young people discover their gifts from God that they can use to make the world a better place and themselves better individuals.

The place of the physical in life is part of that learning. Youth learn to accept their sexuality as a beautiful and essential part of their personality but not the sole way of expressing their vitality. They observe lives wrecked by a false sense of values. And, by the grace of God, they choose a life of devotion to Christ in which they are fully sexual, fully masculine or feminine, always trying to become more open and mature. They learn that possessing material goods does not insure happiness. With deeper understanding of what is essential in life when they enter marriage, they are ready for the new challenges, the pleasure and pain, and opportunities for growth that that special relationship offers. They also learn that some are called to the single life and can move toward that in a chaste, celibate manner.

Religious Life

Taking a vow of chastity as a member of a religious order or secular institute is a way of reminding others that God's love is available to all. A religious does not have the previous commitment to one person in marriage. Therefore, he or she can be available to anyone in need. Love in marriage is a sign of how particularly God loves us. Love given by those vowed to virginity is a sign of how universally God loves us. The Church needs both reminders.

Joining a youth group associated with the Secular Franciscan Order is another way to find people who share Christian ideals, who work for justice in the world and who have a lot of fun doing it!

Questions for Reflection—What is the fundamental attitude of the virtue of chastity whether for the married or unmarried? What are the values that wholesome activities bring to young people? Is sexuality "added" to human personality or is it an essential ingredient? Why is chastity emphasized in speaking of young people?

Connecting With Scripture and Franciscan Writings—Salvation through

Christ, duties of Christians in Romans, Chapters 5-8, 12, 13. Bodo, pp. 57-60.

Application to Daily Life—Should the ideals of the Christian be so clear that others can sense them? How can you form your conscience about movies, books and the like? What is the purpose of dating? Pray for the grace to be respectful of yourself and others whether in the married, unmarried or not-yet-married life.

Prayer—O, God, guide me in a way of life that will reveal to young people I meet the joy of living in your Spirit. Fill me with true love rather than lust, desire to serve you rather than myself and the courage to live by your laws rather than the world's temptations. Amen.

REFLECTION 22

Obedience

"The Rule and Life of the Lesser Brothers is this: to observe the Holy Gospel of Our Lord Jesus Christ by living in obedience, without anything of one's own, and in chastity.

"Brother Francis promises obedience and reverence to our Lord Pope Honorius and his successors canonically elected and to the Roman Church. Let the other brothers be bound to obey Brother Francis and his successors."

—Saint Francis, The Later Rule

The Foundation

Saint Francis founded an order of brothers. But he founded it on the rock of obedience for two important reasons: 1) that by absolute and unquestioning loyalty to the Church, the order might avoid the shipwreck of heresy into which other movements fell; 2) that his brothers and sisters might have, with poverty and chastity, the third great means of purifying and liberating self-denial—the giving up of one's own will under a Rule.

Secular Franciscans do not, of course, take a vow of obedience. The Rule and Constitutions do not, of themselves, bind under pain of sin. But, by their spirit of obedience, all Secular Franciscans can benefit from the counsel of obedience.

Obedience to the Church

It was said of Saint Francis and his friend, Saint Dominic, that they were always on the road to Rome or from Rome for the Pope's approval on their work. The brothers and sisters of Saint Francis must never forget that they are Catholic before they are Franciscans. Rather, the better Franciscans they are, the better Catholics they will be.

The Holy Father

The Rule of the Secular Franciscan Order reminds us that the Order "adapts...to the needs and expectations of the Holy Church.... Its interpretation belongs to the Holy See." Secular Franciscans should pray for the Pope, love and obey him as the rock of unity and permanence of the Church.

Bishops and Priests

Bishops are the successors of the Apostles. One of the striking characteristics of Saint Francis's life was his great humility and docility in dealing with bishops and priests. Even when he might have criticized, or when priests were evidently not doing their duty, Francis maintained a great reverence for the clergy. He did not choose to win any battles with anyone—except to win their love by his extreme kindness and humility. A Secular Franciscan should be interested, as a member of the Mystical Body of Christ, in his diocese and parish, and is called to cooperate with his bishop and pastor.

In the Order

The workings of the organization of the Secular Franciscan Order are explained later in the book. Suffice it to say here that every member should try to have the particularly Franciscan "obedience of charity" so much praised by Saint Francis. In the matter of attending meetings, holding office, contributing to the spiritual and material welfare of the Order, cooperating in the work of the Apostolic Commissions, the obedience of Secular Franciscans should imitate the humility and charity of Saint Francis.

The Spirit of Obedience

Obedience is not merely a necessity of organization. It possesses two grace-full purposes. First, obedience provides a means of self-denial and self-giving. Poverty strives for freedom from greed. Chastity seeks perfect reasonableness in the sacred area of sex. Obedience seeks freedom from all stubbornness, selfishness, self-centeredness. Obedience calls one to exercise self-discipline, to cooperate and obey according to the Rule and Constitutions. This effort will have one great result: release from self-seeking and pride.

Giving of Oneself by Obedience

Another way of looking at obedience of vow or spirit is to realize that it means simply "giving oneself to the cause." This cause is the Church's mission to live and preach the gospel. By obedience we make ourselves available to the Church for whatever she might call us to perform.

Crisis and Criticism

The whole world suffers an "authority crisis." Partly because of the instantaneous and detailed broadcasting of all the faults of authority, partly because of a greater sense of the value and freedom of each individual, it is difficult for anyone in authority to have credibility and influence. This points to a great need for responsible people to lead the way in sincere and respectful cooperation with authority.

At the same time, one need not be mindless or thoughtless to be obedient. A healthy, honest expression of opinion is welcomed by any mature person in authority. No one is all-wise. We need each other's ideas, encouragement and just criticism. We learn from them. We grow from them.

Questions for Reflection—How does obedience compare with poverty and chastity? What two purposes can obedience have?

Connecting With Scripture and Franciscan Writings—Purity and marriage, the Eucharist in 1 Corinthians, Chapter 6:12-20, Chapter 7, Chapter 11:17-34, Chapters 12-15. Bodo, pp. 61-65.

Application to Daily Life—What authority do you have most difficulty obeying? What is the prudent way to make suggestions to those in authority? Can you think of a synonym for obedience? Try to make one positive suggestion to someone in authority—in your family, in the Church, the state, or in your own Secular Franciscan community.

Prayer—I need a gentled spirit, Lord, if I find myself wrestling with what the Church teaches. Keep me mindful that this is your Church. You are its head. You will keep it in your care. Make me an obedient follower. Amen.

Prayer

*P*rayer is the God-given means by which
we move on our spiritual journeys of life.
We may commit the entire Holy Bible to
memory. We may read ponderous volumes
about Francis, Clare, other saints, Church
history. We may do good works that bring
joy to the world. But, if we do not pray,
we miss the intimate relationship with
God that we are promised. Jesus said,
"I am the way, and the truth, and the life.
No one comes to the Father except through
me" (John 14:6). We go to God through
Jesus, through prayer. The following
reflections may help you deepen and
expand your prayer life. Wherever you
are in your prayer life is a good beginning.
Now Jesus challenges you to desire more
from prayer. Be prepared to give and to
receive more, much more.

REFLECTION 23

The Spirit and Practice of Prayer

"Saint Francis became a living prayer"
—*Celano*, The Life of Saint Francis

"Man achieves the fullness of prayer not when he expresses himself, but when he lets God be most fully present in prayer. The history of mystical prayer...attests to this: Saint Francis, Saint Teresa of Avila, Saint John of the Cross...."

—*Pope John Paul II*, Crossing the Threshold of Hope

Working at Love

Overcrowded divorce courts are tragic proof of the fact that people who fell "in love" can fall "out of love." No matter how much we would like to think that love "just naturally" bubbles on forever like a fountain, the hard fact of life is that love rather resembles a garden. Gardens require hard work to flourish. They must be nurtured, weeded, watered. Working in the garden of love may be called prayer. This is not a very romantic definition but is one born of the experience of human weakness.

People who fall out of love—presuming they really were in love in the first place—are those who neglect to cultivate real intimacy. Husbands and wives may be very busy doing things that presumably express love—fixing up a home, getting kids to school or music lessons or soccer practice, repairing, saving, hurrying from task to task—but, if they do not stop in their hurried life to simply sit down with each other in quiet but real communion of feelings, they are on a dead-end road.

So it is with our relationship with the God we cannot see. We can be very busy serving God, but if we do not work at a simple intimacy on a regular basis, we will also end up in a real or equivalent "divorce" from God.

No Clocks, Please

We would like to say in our own defense, "But, my whole life is a prayer! Why worry about some particular part of it?" That's an attractive temptation. It can gain support from Saint Francis' famous phrase, "the *spirit* of prayer and devotion, to which all temporal things must be subservient." But the analogy of marriage is still true; wives and husbands wear themselves out doing all sorts of busy things "for" each other and the family. But if this supposedly healthy exterior is not nourished regularly by personal communion, it may become a substitute—or a flight from—real love.

Prayer is praying and nothing else. Prayer is not "offering up" our dish-washing, grass-cutting, snow-shoveling and tire-changing. Prayer is looking at God, listening to God, responding to God *and to nothing else*. This means that there must be portions of our day when there is prayer and *nothing else*.

The Purpose of Prayer

Having argued (perhaps at too great length) for times of prayer, we may be more ready to take seriously the purpose and value of prayer. Let's take a broad view.

Prayer is simply the response of the human person to the personal approach of God. It doesn't treat God like some far-off president or potentate to whom we dutifully pay taxes in return for the benefits of citizenship. Prayer rises above the temptation to think that God has so many children that he couldn't possibly be interested in me. Prayer believes—perhaps with difficulty—that God wants a personal relationship with me that is unique, totally different from all the other relationships God has. My relationship with God depends on how I manage my relationships with others. But, at the heart of my life is the call to personal intimacy with God, my Father, my Mother, my Creator. God made me for himself. I achieve that purpose by receiving God—not mechanically, but consciously, willingly, reverently and joyfully.

The Ingredients of Prayer

What, then, is prayer? It is two things. Prayer is our uniquely personal response to God's constant offer of himself. Prayer is a response that is separated from the rest of our lives in order that it may be the soul of the rest of our lives. Prayer is praying and nothing else. Prayer is direct communion with God.

Once this concept is established, we have almost an infinite number of choices as to the details. This is not saying that all roads then lead to the center; rather, it's saying that once the center is taken care of, all roads from the center lead to God.

The first word in prayer can be "I" but a more polite beginning is "you." The focus is placed on God. Saint Francis gives us a perfect example of this in his *Praises of God*.

> *"You are the **holy** Lord God Who does **wonderful things**.*
> *You are strong. You are great. You are the most high.*
>
> *. . .*
>
> *You are love, charity; You are wisdom, you are humility,*
>
> *. . .*
>
> *You are beauty, You are meekness....*
>
> *Our happiness consists in praising the glory and goodness of God:*
> *We give you thanks for your great glory."*

The second word may be "I." "I admit my sin, my weakness. I believe in your mercy. I open myself to your healing. I trust you. I am convinced that your presence and strength within me is the source of all holiness. I ask you confidently for all I need: for the health and welfare of my friends and enemies, for peace and justice, for your Church. for the salvation of the world."

Questions for Reflection—What is essential to any personal relationship? What is prayer? How has your prayer changed over the years?

Connecting With Scripture and Franciscan Writings—Canticle of the three young men in Daniel, Chapter 3. Bodo, pp. 66-68; Normile, *Following Francis of Assisi*, Chapter 9.

Application to Daily Life—What should be the first word spoken in prayer? How does God enter into our prayer? If you are not already doing so, set aside a definite time for prayer in your day, perhaps as soon as you get up, or whatever time is best for quiet.

Prayer—Help me to remember and to live Saint Francis's words, O God, that if I am upset for any reason whatever, I should immediately rise up to prayer and remain in the presence of the Most High Father for as long as it takes you to restore me to the joy of my salvation. Amen.

From the Rule of the Secular Franciscan Order

8. As Jesus was the true worshiper of the Father, so let prayer and contemplation be the soul of all they are and do.

   Let them participate in the sacramental life of the Church, above all the Eucharist. Let them join in liturgical prayer in one of the forms proposed by the Church, reliving the mysteries of the life of Christ.

Praying With God's Word

"With an imploring gaze upon the holy countenance of Jesus, Francis uttered the following prayer: 'Great and glorious God, my Lord Jesus Christ! I implore you to enlighten me and to disperse the darkness of my soul! Give me true faith and firm hope and a perfect charity! Grant me, O Lord, to know you so well that in all things I may act by your light, and in accordance with your holy will.'"

—Jorgensen, Life of St. Francis

Using the Scriptures

The presence of Jesus is not limited to the appearances of bread and wine. With God and the Holy Spirit, he is present everywhere—but, in a most personal way to his brothers and sisters, good and bad. God speaks to us by many means—the voices and examples of others, our own experience of grace and sin, the beauty and mystery of nature, but in a particular way, God speaks to us in his inspired Word, the Scriptures. Vatican II reminded us of the presence of Christ when the Scriptures are read in Church. We may be sure of a particularly power-ful presence when we take up his words with reverence.

The Books of the Bible

Bible study is not prayer but preparation for prayer. However, some acquaintance with the background of the various books of the Bible is essential to a fruitful use of it in prayer. It is to be hoped that Secular Franciscans will use the opportunities offered in Bible study groups or form their own Scripture study group. If one wants to study privately, inexpensive pamphlets of commentary on all the individual books of the Bible are available under the title, *New Testament Reading Guide(s)* and *Old Testament Reading Guide(s)* or *Scripture from Scratch*, St. Anthony Messenger Press. Here we can do little more than give a very simple overview of the whole Bible:

    I. The New Testament (27 Books)

      A) Four Gospels: Matthew, Mark, Luke, John

B) The Acts of the Apostles: the story of the early Church

C) Letters of Paul, James, Peter, John and Jude, spelling out the meaning of Jesus' life, death, Resurrection and exaltation

D) The Book of Revelation (The Apocalypse): hope in persecution

II. The Old Testament (also known as the Hebrew Scriptures, 46 Books)

A) The Pentateuch (first five books, also called the Torah or the Law)—God saves and establishes his people: Genesis, Exodus, Leviticus, Numbers and Deuteronomy; plus Joshua, Judges, Ruth (total 8 books)

B) The Historical Books show God's plan operating: First and Second Samuel, First and Second Kings, First and Second Chronicles, Ezra, Nehemiah, Tobit, Judith, Esther, First and Second Maccabees (13 books)

C) The wisdom literature, practical approaches to the problems of life, with poetry and prayer: Job, the Psalms, Proverbs, Ecclesiastes, Song of Songs, Wisdom, Sirach (7 books)

D) The Prophets, the "conscience of Israel:" Isaiah, Jeremiah, Lamentations, Baruch, Ezekiel, Daniel, Hosea, Joel, Amos, Obadiah, Jonah, Micah, Nahum, Habakkuk, Zephaniah, Haggai, Zechariah, Malachi (18 books)

A total of seventy-three books comprise the "library" which we call the Holy Bible.

Several good translations of the Bible are available. Two excellent choices are: 1) *The New American Bible*, published in 1987; 2) *The Jerusalem Bible*, published in 1966.

Prayer Is Not Study

The study of the Bible is one good thing; prayer is another. When you use the Bible to pray, you are simply going to listen to God with an open mind and heart. You believe God is now speaking to you personally. Perhaps you need to use your mind to understand what the human words actually meant at the time the Scriptures were written but prayer is no time to worry over or be distracted by problems of authorship, history, grammar or varying opinions.

Read calmly, slowly, prayerfully. Have a plan, but do not try to make so many "yards" a day. For instance, you may be praying the

Gospel of Saint Matthew. Studying the book may take you six months. Praying it may take you six years—or a lifetime. Simply take a verse or two or as many as you need, and listen to what God is saying to you in your circumstances today. What is God calling you to be or to do? What acts of God are being illuminated? What reality in your own life—good or bad—is God pointing out? What motivation is being instilled in you?

This method of praying Scripture is sometimes called *lectio divina*. *Lectio divina* consists of four steps and while seemingly simple, the process does take time.

Read. Read a passage of Scripture slowly, thoughtfully, perhaps aloud.

Reflect. Ask what the Scripture has to say to you at this particular time in your life. What is God saying to you through the Scripture?

Respond. How does the Scripture make you feel? Are you willing to act as God seems to be directing you or do you sense your own resistance? Talk to God about your response.

Receive. Sit back quietly with the Scriptures and the message they have brought and be prepared to receive what God has for you. The insights, the inspirations, the challenges that come to you are God's gift. Receive that gift with a grateful heart.

God Speaks, We Respond

Now, you cannot write a script for lovers, though Hollywood and television try. Each two people express their relationship in their own unique words and silences, looks, gestures, posture, action, being. So it is with God and us. There is no script for anyone to follow. There are general directions (see Reflection 25), but each of us responds according to our own personal makeup. Some are more emotionally enthusiastic than others. Some pray longer than others. Some are imaginative. Others are more formal. But in every case, real prayer means facing the reality of God with pure heart and mind and giving the human response that truth lighted by the Spirit demands.

The Gospels, the Rule of Our Life

Francis was a man whom God led to almost an ecstatic reverence for the Word of God. The Bible was the source of his original inspiration. His first Rule was a collection of Bible texts. When he could not attend daily Mass, he had the Gospel of the day read to him from the missal. He said, "If I cannot be present at Mass, I adore the Body of Christ in meditation and with the eyes of the soul, in like manner as if I were present at Mass."

Questions for Reflection—Can you identify the four major divisions of the New Testament? The same for the Old? How can the Scriptures be used for prayer? What is the difference between studying the Bible and *lectio divina*?

Connecting With Scripture and Franciscan Writings—Jesus' prayer at the Last Supper in John 17. Bodo, pp. 68-71.

Application to Daily Life—Reflect on a situation in your life that calls for decision-making. As you pray the Scriptures, ask God for wisdom in reaching a wise decision for that situation. You might keep a journal of your experience of praying with the Word of God. Select a brief passage from Scripture and pray that Scripture each day, noting the insights that develop from your prayer.

Prayer—I will rejoice in you, Lord, always. I will rejoice because I know your kindness and want to share it with others. You are near. I will not worry but in everything through prayer with thanksgiving, I will make my needs known to you. I claim your peace, O God, the peace that passes all human understanding because you guard my heart and mind. In Jesus' name, amen (from Philippians 4:4-7).

A Method of Praying

"With an imploring gaze upon the holy countenance of Jesus, Francis uttered the following prayer: 'Great and glorious God, my Lord Jesus Christ! I implore Thee to enlighten me and to disperse the darkness of my soul! Give me true faith and firm hope and a perfect charity! Grant me, O Lord, to know Thee so well that in all things I may act by Thy light, and in accordance with Thy holy will!'"

—*Jorgensen*, Life of St. Francis

Meditation should not become an intellectual exercise, a study period or a complicated process that supposedly produces a grace-full result. Meditation is a method, but it's anybody's method. It can be yours. Meditation is best done by those who are childlike, sincere and humble.

Meditation is simply the prayer that originates in our own minds and hearts as compared with set prayers that others have given us or written, for example, printed acts of faith, hope, charity. Meditation is informal, even though it may follow a general plan. Meditation is like the conversation of a child with a father or mother: perfectly open, trusting, simple, and filled with a great desire to please God.

A Method

This kind of prayer involves a bit of knowledge that it may be well done:

1) *Create favorable circumstances.* Select a period of time—ten, fifteen minutes, a half hour, an hour—when you will not ordinarily be disturbed. For many people this means early in the morning before the day begins to bustle. Be faithful to the time, no matter how you feel or what activities may threaten this time. It has been said that God redeems the time committed in prayer.

2) *Ask the Holy Spirit to help you to be open to his light and warmth.* Believe in the loving presence of this Gift of God through Jesus and expect the grace of God to heal and recreate you. Sit expectantly in that Presence.

3) Slowly read a passage of Scripture. You're not trying to "get through" a chapter. Perhaps one verse is enough. Place yourself within the scene in your imagination, if possible. Think of Jesus saying the words to you, doing these things for you. Note especially his feelings, how he sees and responds to God's will through his attitudes and reactions to the situation. As you read, stop, perhaps soon, perhaps only after a time, and talk to our Lord about what you have read—what he is saying to you personally. Prayer is your response to the Lord. You experience truth; you hear Christ speaking to you in it. You respond. That is prayer.

4) *Some people are helped by writing their thoughts and responses on paper.* You may want to keep your thoughts in a notebook or journal that's for you alone.

AN EXAMPLE:

Text: "I am the vine, you are the branches. Those who abide in me and I in them bear much fruit, because apart from me you can do nothing" (John 15:5).

Question: How shall I "remain" in Christ? How can I do what Christ would have done or said? In a particular instance? Examples: a) George wanted to take revenge against someone who had wronged him. He thought of Christ on the cross, forgiving, and he chose not to take revenge. b) Mary is on her way out the door. Her mother calls her back to do a small chore. She thinks of the patient Christ as she returns. c) A nurse must care for a cantankerous patient. She thinks of Christ's healing and consoling ways and smiles lovingly at the patient. d) Jim listens patiently, just as Christ listened, to someone with a long tale of woe.

More examples: a) You are sick, in pain, tired, annoyed. It is an opportunity to 'fill up in your body for what is wanting in the sufferings of Christ.' b) You are tempted to envy the person telling you about her great success. You remember that Christ could have changed everything in a second but he accepted life as it was. c) You are reading an interesting book when someone interrupts you to ask for your help. You remember that "Christ arose and followed them" when they came to him for help. d) You see people walking down the street and remember that Christ walked the roads of Galilee. You see Christ in the people walking in your town.

Christ's Presence

Gradually, Christ becomes more vivid to us. By trying to live like him, we learn to love him more. Certain aspects of his person begin to answer our deepest desires. We are not merely discovering the beauty of a truth, we are learning to love a person. Christ becomes someone living and present. I am not simply following him. The more detailed the comparison between Christ's life and mine, the more I can say, "I live, now not I, but Christ lives in me." That's what Francis did. That's what we are called to do.

Response

Perhaps it is good to emphasize again that your response is your prayer. How will you respond? It depends on circumstances. You may feel love, hatred, joy or sorrow. Desire, anger, fear or hope, shame, determination, trust or humility may flood you. We react in many ways to God's truth.

Your response may be delight, admiration, adoration, thanksgiving. Or begging, apology, peace or generosity. Whatever your response, let it go whole-heartedly and honestly to Christ, your brother. If you have only one of these feelings or attitudes for half an hour, it doesn't matter. Just be yourself; be a child, trust God.

Above all, remember this. Your prayer really does not depend on how successful you are. You may feel miserable. God may seem to be a million miles away. God will accept your prayer not on the basis of how you feel but because you've reached out in prayer.

5) *Finally, you'll want to end your prayer time properly.* Conclude your prayer with "Thank you, God, for helping me to pray." Then make a little resolution, just one, to help you love God more. Just keep doing these things and your prayer will be an offering pleasing to God. And your life will become quite different!

Questions for Reflection—Describe meditation as simply as you can. What word best describes prayer?

Connecting With Scripture and Franciscan Writings—The second coming of Christ in 1 and 2 Thessalonians. Bodo, pp. 72-76.

Application to Daily Life—What is the best time for you to pray? Jot down a few words to help you keep in mind a simple method of prayer. Decide to set aside some special time for prayer every day and be faithful to it no matter how you feel.

Prayer—Lord, I often pray with many words. Now I offer you my prayer of listening silence in your holy presence.... Amen.

REFLECTION 26

Christ Joins Us to His Prayer: The Liturgy

"And the Lord gave me such faith in churches that I would pray with simplicity in this way and say: 'We adore You, Lord Jesus Christ, in all Your churches throughout the whole world, and we bless You because by Your holy cross You have redeemed the world.'"

—*Saint Francis*, The Testament

What Is Liturgy?

At the pinnacle of creation is Christ, the Perfect Adorer of God, the Perfect Lover of God, the Perfect Prayer. The Son of God united himself personally to one human nature. Thus united to all creation, he has united himself mystically to all who open themselves to his call. He continues his saving work today through the Body which he gathers around him, the Church. Through this action, Christ continues his prayer, his offering, his healing, his giving of life.

Every liturgical celebration (Eucharist, other sacraments, the Liturgy of the Hours, sacramentals) is an action of Christ the priest, and of his Body, the Church. In the liturgy, full public worship is performed by the Mystical Body of Jesus, by the head and his members.

Christ always associates the Church with himself in the truly great work of giving perfect praise to God and making people holy. The Church is his dearly beloved bride who calls to her Lord and through him offers worship to the eternal Father.

Christ is always present in his Church but especially in her liturgical celebrations. He is present in the sacrifice of the Mass, not only in the person of his priest (Jesus who once offered himself on the cross continues the sacrifice through the ministry of his priests) but especially under the appearances of bread and wine. He is present by his power in the sacraments so that when a human being baptizes, it is really Christ himself who baptizes. He is present in his word since it is he himself who speaks when the holy Scriptures are read in the Church. He is present, finally, when the Church prays and sings, for he promised:

"[W]here two or three are gathered in my name, I am there among them" (Matthew 18:20).

The preceding three paragraphs are taken substantially from Vatican II's great document on the liturgy. Vatican II reminded us that the liturgy is the outstanding means by which the faithful can express in their lives and manifest to others the *mystery of Christ* and the *real nature of the Church*.

The *"mystery of Christ"* is that he reveals the mercy of God in human nature and saves us by his loving life, death and Resurrection. The real "nature of the Church is that it is consciously, freely, responsibly joined to Christ in his work. The Church is the sign or sacrament of Christ in the world today. We can no longer see him, yet we must continue to see him. He is visible in his Church—a Body of people joined together, not merely by being physically next to each other in a building, but united in his grace, consciously feeling and exercising their responsibility to each other and to the world.

The Eucharist

The Mass then is many things. The celebration of the Eucharist makes present the saving sacrifice of Christ. In it Christ joins his people into one worshiping Body. It is the Body of Christ—individuals freely joining others—accepting the salvation of Christ. The Mass is Christ worshiping, the Church worshiping with him.

The key word is "Church." Church is not some far-off abstraction— "over there" somewhere. Church is not the Pope and the bishops. It is not the especially holy people. Church is all of us, who by the grace of God voluntarily accept the call of Christ to be saved through him as members of his Body. We are the Church!

This is not an arbitrary or merely functional arrangement. It is in the very nature of things: *I cannot love God without loving my neighbor, and vice versa.* I cannot love God as a human being without expressing this love through my body, *visibly, externally.* So the Mass, and all liturgy, expresses both my union with God and with my neighbor. *Church is, therefore, a community or social matter and also a visible, external, public matter.* Its purpose is to indicate that all that we do as Christians is ultimately directed to the praise of God with Christ our brother.

Questions for Reflection—Who acts in the liturgy? What is the real nature of the Church? Why must worship be communal and public as well as private?

Connecting With Scripture and Franciscan Writings—The Priesthood of Christ in Hebrews, Chapter 4:14-16, Chapters 5, 6, 10, 12, 13. Bodo, pp. 77-79.

Application to Daily Life—Are you ready to accept the call to "full, active and conscious participation" in the liturgy? Do you feel it is your "right and duty" to participate? Each time you share in the celebration of the Mass, try to consciously realize the various ways of participating in the liturgy: "acclamations, responses, psalmody, antiphons, songs, actions, gestures, bodily attitudes, reverent silence."

Prayer—Oh, God, I praise and thank you for being our God of celebration who gathers us as a people in your name. I long to experience you in worship and in my fellow Christians. Thank you for the privilege of being one among many who love you. Amen.

Eucharist: Contemplating the Mystery

"As He revealed Himself to the holy apostles in true flesh, so He reveals Himself to us now in sacred bread. And as they saw only His flesh by an insight of their flesh, yet believed that He was God as they contemplated Him with their spiritual eyes, let us, as we see bread and wine with our bodily eyes, see and firmly believe that they are His most holy Body and Blood living and true.

—Saint Francis, Admonition I

Contemplating the Mystery

Because the Eucharist is a "mystery," that is, it reveals as well as conceals God, we will never penetrate the full depth of its beauty. Christ gave us this mystery so that he could "perpetuate the sacrifice of the Cross throughout the centuries until he comes again." In the words of the liturgy itself: "O holy banquet, in which Christ is received, the memory of his Passion is renewed, our spirit is filled with grace, and a pledge of future glory is given us."

Points for Meditation

The Mass is over in a relatively short time. We can scarcely become aware of even one of the great meanings before us, still less all of them. The following considerations are offered for meditation, for preparation and thanksgiving after Mass. Perhaps one a day will be helpful. (They are taken from *Christian Commitment* by Father Karl Rahner.)

What we do at Mass:

1. We utter with Christ his high priestly thanksgiving for creation and redemption. We have received, each in our own way, a share in the priesthood of Christ and we are able to stand before God and speak the thanksgiving of the whole world for his love and mercy.

2. We enter freely into our Lord's own love made present to unite us.

We accept it. We experience it for others. This is not a self-manufactured love we offer. We share it in the love that Jesus has for his Father. The Eucharist makes this visibly present to us so that we may enter into it.

3. *We celebrate the death of the Lord.* To "celebrate" is to "perform, do." We are made present to the life-giving death and Resurrection of Jesus.

4. *We surrender ourselves to the weakness and vulnerability of man,* our present subjection to death and evil, as the circumstances in which God's power works in us. We cannot save ourselves from the tragedy of sin that has blighted the whole human race. We accept ourselves as a sinful race called to the redemption that only God can achieve.

5. *We give our personal consent to the obedience with which Jesus died for us.* We are not saved automatically even if the whole power of our salvation comes from Christ. We must pray for the gift to say "Yes!" freely, gladly, wholeheartedly. "Our desire to thank you is your gift."

6. *We renew our Lord's consent to the cross and death as the law of our own life.* To live is to die to all that is not God, to die to all selfishness and self-sufficiency. To live is to be conscious and free with the power of the Spirit.

7. We enter into the forgiveness of sins won by Christ's saving death and Resurrection. We accept forgiveness and offer it to others. The Eucharist is forgiveness. It is the sign of God's lifting us up from death and breathing his Spirit into us.

8. We enter into the victory of Christ in his Resurrection and glorification. We are already participants. Our life is a tension between the "already"—we already are in Christ, marked for resurrection—and the "not yet"—the full sharing in victory.

9. We celebrate the Resurrection and glorification of the Lord. It was not just his death that saved us. Inseparable from the cross, like the other side of the same coin, Jesus' glorious Resurrection is the Father's promise to us also.

10. *We say "yes" to the new covenant sealed by the Blood of Christ.* God has entered into a solemn pact with us as the Body of Christ. He is our God and we are his people.

11. *We enter into the coming of the Kingdom.* The Kingdom is God possessing us in love. It is our freely opening ourselves to God's love. The

Kingdom comes through Christ. It becomes visible through the Church, the sign lifted up among the nations.

12. *We ratify the transformation and forgiveness of the world which began with Christ's death and Resurrection.* We are not passive spectators of salvation. We enter into the plan that lived in the heart of God from eternity.

13. *We look forward with confidence, hope, expectation to the coming of Christ.* Judgment should be something we welcome, a declaration that we have accepted Christ and live his life. We have perhaps a natural fear of death, but we are also confident and eager to see Christ. Come, Lord Jesus!

14. *We receive the Body and Blood of Christ as a sign of the grace we have received and the grace we shall receive.* There is no more perfect sacrament or sign of the love of God than this: he gives us himself in actual bodily union. He gives his whole being—God and man, soul and body. He has no rest until his whole being—divinity and humanity—is joined to our whole being. God actually wants to be united to us.

Saint Francis

As we meditate on these profound mysteries, we may be moved to say with Saint Francis: "O sublime lowliness, O low sublimity! That the Lord of the universe, God and the Son of God, should so humble himself as to hide under the tiny little form of bread for our welfare. Look, brothers, at the humility of God and pour out your hearts before him. Be humble yourselves so that you may be exalted by him."

Questions for Reflection—Why is the Mass a mystery? What is the first purpose of the Mass?

Connecting With Scripture and Franciscan Writings—Patience, a living faith, in the Letter of James. Bodo, pp. 79-81.

Application to Daily Life—Which of the many aspects of the Mass is most meaningful to you? How is all of life, not just the few minutes of Mass, "eucharist" or "thanksgiving?" Pray for deeper understanding of the true meaning of the Mass. Allow what you experience at Mass to change your approach to daily living.

Prayer—"My God and my all" (Saint Francis).

The Liturgy of the Hours

"And so I beseech the Minister General, my superior, to see that the Rule is observed faithfully by all, and that the clerics say the Office devoutly, not concentrating on the melody of the chants, but being careful that their hearts are in harmony—so that their words may be in harmony with their hearts—and their hearts with God. Their aim should be to please God by purity of heart, not to soothe the ears of the congregation by their sweet singing."

—*Saint Francis,* Letter to a General Chapter

The Liturgy of the Hours

At the mandate of Vatican II, the Liturgy of the Hours (Breviary, Divine Office) was revised. In the General Instruction we find these words: "Whenever possible, other groups of the faithful (besides bishops, priests, clergy) should come together in Church to celebrate the principal hours of the liturgy. Since parishes 'in a certain way represent the visible Church as it is established throughout the world,' they could celebrate the principal hours publicly in Church whenever it is possible."

The Secular Franciscan Order Liturgy of the Hours

Secular Franciscans have several choices in saying the daily Divine Office: 1) Morning and evening prayer from the Liturgy of the Hours or a shortened form of the same; 2) the Little Office of the Blessed Virgin Mary; 3) the Office of the Passion by Saint Francis of Assisi; 4) the Office of the Twelve Our Fathers; 5) other forms of liturgical prayer containing psalms, Scripture reading and prayers; 6) special prayer forms of the liturgical seasons such as the Way of the Cross, the Rosary or Franciscan Crown (See *Ritual of the Secular Franciscan Order*, pp. 103-104).

Importance of the Liturgy of the Hours

The Liturgy of the Hours is the prayer of the Church. It is not, therefore, a private prayer, even when said by one person. Like all liturgy, it is the prayer of Christ and his Body carried throughout the whole day. We can do no better than quote from the "General Instruction" of The Liturgy of the Hours:

The public and communal prayer of the people of God is truly one of the primary responsibilities of the Church. From the very beginning, the baptized "devoted themselves to the apostles' instruction and the communal life, to the breaking of bread and the prayers" (Acts 2:42). The Acts of the Apostles give frequent testimony to the fact that the Christian community prayed with one accord (Acts 1:14; 4:24; 12:5,12 and Ephesians 5:19-21). The witness of the early Church teaches us that individual Christians devoted themselves to prayer at fixed times...the custom soon grew to assigning special times to common prayer,...the last hour of the day, when evening draws on and the lamp is lighted, or the first hours, when night draws to a close with the rising of the day star. In the course of time other hours came to be sanctified by common prayer...This Liturgy of the Hours...enriched by readings, is principally a prayer of praise and petition. In fact, it is the prayer of the Church with Christ and to Christ. (The Liturgy of the Hours, Vol. 1, pp. 21-22)

The Prayer of Christ

Christ Jesus, high priest of the new and eternal covenant, took our human nature and introduced into the world of our exile that hymn of praise which is sung in the heavenly places throughout all ages. From then on the praise of God wells up from the heart of Christ in human words of adoration, propitiation and intercession, presented to the Father by the head of the new humanity, the mediator between God and mankind, in the name of all and for the good of all. (The Liturgy of the Hours, Vol. 1, p. 22)

The Church Continues the Prayer of Christ

The excellence of Christian prayer lies in this, that it shares in the very love of the only-begotten Son for the Father and in that prayer which the Son put into words in his earthly life and which still continues unceasingly in the name of the whole human race and for its salvation, throughout the universal Church and in all its members. (The Liturgy of the Hours, Vol. 1, p. 26)

The Action of the Holy Spirit

It is this Spirit who "helps us in our weakness" and "intercedes for us with longings too deep for words" (Romans 8:26). (The Liturgy of the Hours, Vol. 1, p. 27)

The Communal Nature of Prayer

...[T]here is a special excellence in the prayer of the community.

Christ himself has said: "Where two or three are gathered together in my name, I am there in their midst" (Matthew 18:20). (The Liturgy of the Hours, Vol. 1, p. 28)

The Eucharist and the Liturgy of the Hours
The Liturgy of the Hours extends to the different hours of the day the praise and thanksgiving, the commemoration of the mysteries of salvation, the petitions and the foretaste of heavenly glory, that are present in the eucharistic mystery.... The Liturgy of the Hours is an excellent preparation for the celebration of the Eucharist itself, for it inspires and deepens in a fitting way the dispositions necessary for the fruitful celebration of the Eucharist: faith, hope, love, devotion and the spirit of self-denial. (The Liturgy of the Hours, Vol. 1, p. 29)

Praise Given to God in Union With the Church in Heaven
In the Liturgy of the Hours, the Church exercises the priestly office of its head and offers to God "unceasingly" a sacrifice of praise.... This prayer is "the voice of the bride herself as she addresses the bridegroom; indeed, it is also the prayer of Christ and his body to the Father." All therefore who offer this prayer are fulfilling a duty of the Church, and also sharing in the highest honor given to Christ's bride, because as they render praise to God they are standing before God's throne in the name of Mother Church. (The Liturgy of the Hours, Vol. 1, p. 30)

Supplication and Intercession
Besides the praise of God, the Church in the Liturgy of the Hours expresses the prayers and desires of all the Christian faithful; indeed, it prays to Christ, and through him to the Father, for the salvation of the whole world. The voice of the Church is not just its own; it is also the voice of Christ, that is, "through our Lord Jesus Christ," and so the Church continues to offer the prayer and petition which Christ poured out in the days of his earthly life. (The Liturgy of the Hours, Vol. 1, p. 31-32)

Saint Francis
The Liturgy of the Hours is another way the Church gives us to heed the words of Saint Francis that we are to work in such a way that we "do not extinguish the spirit of prayer and devotion, to which all temporal things must be subordinate."

Questions for Reflection—Who may celebrate the Liturgy of the Hours? Recall the general definition of liturgy. Why is it called the Liturgy of the *Hours*?

Connecting With Scripture and Franciscan Writings—Counsels and warnings from Saint Peter in 1 Peter, Chapters 1-3; 2 Peter, Chapters 2-3. Bodo, pp. 82-86.

Application to Daily Life—How is your praying the Liturgy of the Hours part of the whole prayer of Christ and his Church? As you pray the Liturgy of the Hours, make a special effort to realize your union with Christ and the whole Church. Visualize yourself as an integral part of the faithful praying throughout the world.

Prayer—Come, let us worship the Lord who calls us to be his people. Amen.

REFLECTION 29

*Praying as a Group**

> *"Wherever we are,*
> *in every place,*
> *at very hour,*
> *at very time of the day,*
> *every day and continually,*
> *let all of us truly and humbly believe,*
> *hold in our heart and love,*
> *honor, adore, serve,*
> *praise and bless,*
> *glorify and exalt,*
> *magnify and give thanks*
> *to the Most High and Supreme Eternal God..."*
>
> —*Saint Francis,* Earlier Rule

Midway between the great liturgical prayer of the Church and the private prayer of individuals stands the prayer of a group of persons who voluntarily come together to pray. This form of prayer is less structured, more spontaneous than the prayer of the Mass and other sacraments. Without implying any inferiority of private personal prayer, it merits the special blessing Christ promised: "For where two or three are gathered in my name, I am there among them" (Matthew 18:20). It is no substitute for either liturgical prayer or private prayer yet it can enrich both. As the fruit of private prayer and as preparation for the Eucharist or other sacramental celebration, shared prayer makes obvious the essential community aspect of the Church.

Suggestions for Structured Prayer Time

Many persons are helped by following a certain loose structure for praying together: 1) an opening hymn; 2) silence and recollection; 3) the reading of a psalm, slowly and clearly, as a springboard for continuing

---

* This chapter was developed by Leonard Foley, O.F.M., from observations on shared prayer by Father Bohdan Kosicki and Father George Kosicki, C.S.B., Archdiocese of Detroit.

prayer; 4) response to the psalm by silence, or spontaneous prayer of praise and thanksgiving, or a hymn, or an appropriate Scripture reading; perhaps another psalm read by someone else; 5) the Magnificat or some other hymn may be sung; followed by, 6) prayers of petition by various individuals, extended as long as desired; 7) a closing prayer of thanksgiving to God for hearing our prayers.

Unstructured Is an Option

Other persons may prefer unstructured prayer with no particular psalms or other prayers chosen ahead of time. Two or more simply gather in reverent silence and await the inspiration of the Spirit to guide their prayer.

Essentials

Though prayers of petition are a part of common prayer, the emphasis should be on praise and thanksgiving to the Father in the Spirit of Jesus. The major experience is the presence of Christ praying with the gathered community and this prayer pleases God. Though it is a group prayer, members should pay primary attention not to each other but to the presence of Christ. God- or Christ-centeredness is the heart of the prayer. Shared prayer is heavily based on Scripture. All who come to pray should bring their Bibles.

Silence

When the group is composed of persons who have a habit of prayer, extended moments of silence are frequent. Usually the more mature a group is in prayer, the richer are the silences since all are sharing consciously in the presence of God and the more comfortable the prayers will be with the periods of silence.

Singing

Singing is important. "He who sings well prays twice." Sing with joy. Sing with praise.

Preparation

Shared prayer has a great amount of spontaneity. Yet like anything else worthwhile, it takes preparation. The preparation is the personal prayer and penance of each individual and a serious attempt to be open to the Lord at all times.

It is best to avoid conversation when the group gathers. A time for sharing will come later but the first step is to pay full attention to the presence of God, inviting the Spirit to enlighten and empower the group to praise and thank God. A quiet space to gather, perhaps a lighted candle, an open Bible help to focus the group.

By Their Fruits

The group may know all the mechanics of shared prayer and pray quite well, yet this is not enough. The value of the group's prayer depends on the test each individual must make in his own heart—finding there an ever-deepening personal relationship with Christ and a consequent Christlike love of neighbor.

A Few Don'ts

Shared prayer is not a time for public confession or complaints about the difficulties of life, implicit condemnation of others "piously" prayed for or any other kind of personal ostentation.

A moment does come during the prayer time to speak a prayer of petition for one's personal needs and a time of sharing faith experiences with others. This supports and builds the faith of all the individuals present.

Shared prayer is difficult for many. Some individuals may find it difficult or impossible to pray out loud in their own words before others. This fact should be accepted by the group and no pressure should be put on anyone to "produce." One can pray silently as well as audibly. What is important is that all are praying together in praise of God.

Secular Franciscan Order Prayer Groups

Besides attending the monthly meeting of the whole fraternity, Secular Franciscans are urged to come together in small groups each week to pray. If this is done in the quiet and humble spirit of Saint Francis, they will be immeasurably aided in their whole Christian life.

Questions for Reflection—What is the purpose of shared prayer? How does it relate to our praying at Mass and as individuals?

Connecting With Scripture and Franciscan Writings—The apostle of love in the letters of Saint John. Bodo, pp. 86-90.

Application to Daily Life—Have you experienced the benefit of praying with someone else or having someone pray with you especially in time of sickness or trouble? How might your spiritual life be deepened if you could pray more often with others? Be open to the opportunity to pray with someone else or to join a group for sharing prayer.

Prayer—I ask you, Jesus, for spiritual friends with whom I can gather to be in your presence, to praise you, to talk with you, to listen to you. Enter into our hearts and into our prayers to make us one in you with assurance that we will never face life alone. Amen.

Clare, Bright Light

"She was the first flower in Francis's garden, and she shone like a radiant star, fragrant as a flower blossoming white and pure in springtime."

—Saint Bonaventure

To consider Franciscan life without reflecting on Clare of Assisi is like having a one-sided coin, a song without music, a rainbow without sunshine. Clare was young and in love with life when she witnessed Francis's fervor in following Christ. She might have blushed when she saw Francis, several years her senior, relinquish all he had, even the clothes from his back, to his father, Pietro Bernardone. Perhaps she knew from that moment that she and Francis were spiritual brother and sister because in returning to his earthly father everything he had given him, Francis acknowledged that God in heaven was now his *only* Father. Francis and Clare were lovers also, though not in the usual way the world views lovers, but a man and woman who loved God with their whole hearts and souls and in that love enveloped each other.

Clare's Lesson

What does Clare teach us about following Jesus? She teaches us to follow Francis, who followed Jesus so perfectly and so literally in pursuit of poverty, desiring nothing more than the Lord. Clare teaches us that we can be committed faithful followers of Francis and of Jesus while doing it in our own unique way in accord with our circumstances in life. Both Clare and Francis sacrificed all attachment to material possessions in their search for the Christian life they were called to follow. Francis's journey took him to distant places in his world. He walked hundreds of miles around the peninsula now called Italy. He ventured to the land of the Sultan of Damietta. In contrast Clare journeyed the short distance from her father's home to the little Church of Saint Mary of the Angels, which Francis dubbed the Portiuncula or Little Portion. There she was received by the brothers. After a brief stay with Benedictine nuns, she was to spend the remainder of her life in the convent of San

Damiano, the little chapel where the Lord had spoken to Francis from the crucifix saying, "Go and rebuild my Church."

Clare was to have a permanent home. Francis had special places he visited but if he were alive today, we might say he had no permanent mailing address. Francis met and preached to unknown numbers of people—on the dusty roads, in city squares, in churches and chapels around the countryside, in foreign tents. Clare spread God's love through prayer which attracted followers to her Franciscan way of life. Her prayers brought healings. She wrote letters to those in foreign lands encouraging them in their Franciscan journeys. But she stayed close to home at San Damiano. Two dramatically different life-styles followed the same goal: loving God with all their heart and soul and mind and strength.

Few of us are called to give away everything we possess. In many cases, that might actually be an *un*godly thing to do because we have responsibilities for others—spouses, children, aging parents—that God entrusts to us. God has given us special gifts to use for his purposes—as workers in the marketplace, friends in the community, healers of the brokenhearted, lovers of the downtrodden. We won't shed our clothes on our village square in exchange for a ragged tunic with rope belt as Francis did. We won't have our hair shorn as a sign of humility in imitation of Clare. But we can devote our lives to following Jesus in the way of Francis and Clare in ways adapted to the time in which we live. The challenge of Francis and Clare to us is to discover that way and to persevere on its path in our own times in our own ways.

Quiet Places

Even the twelfth-century hill town of Assisi vibrated with enough noise of humans, animals, carts and wagons to drown the voice of silence. Not only sounds but reminders that there is something we must be *doing* distracts us when we seek God in prayer. Both Clare and Francis sought quiet spots where they could hear the Lord speak in their hearts. They knew God had much to say to them if only they could hear the message. Clare's quiet place was the monastery; Francis retreated to mountain caves.

Our world is undoubtedly much noisier than Assisi of eight centuries ago. Distractions abound. Noise thunders. Even when we think we have discovered a silent space in a pre-dawn early morning, a jet roars overhead or the city garbage trucks begin their routes. Silence is a precious commodity, one to treasure. God has much to say to us, as he did to Clare and Francis, if we can find the space and place to listen.

Images of Clare

Clare's name means "light." She is the bright, shining one who reflected God's love into the world from a cloistered convent where she lived with her spiritual sisters, first known as the Order of Poor Ladies, later Poor Clares. That light continues today to shine through Poor Clares throughout the world as they pray for our world.

Clare is also referred to as the "little plant" of Francis. One can visualize a branch plucked from a plant and stuck in the soil to take root to become a plant of its own. So was Clare's spiritual being rooted in Francis. Both of them were the branches grown from the Lord who proclaimed, "I am the vine, you are the branches" (John 15:5).

Christ is the mirror of God. "Mirror of Perfection" is a term used to describe Francis. And Clare was indeed a mirror of Francis. She caught what he taught by his way of life, then she sent it into the world through her sisters, her prayer, her writing, and the Order she established. You and I can become mirrors of Jesus, Francis and Clare in our own ways, in our own times.

Questions for Reflection—Does Clare's decision to leave her family's home to follow Francis's way seem wise or foolish? What aspect of Clare's way of following Francis and Jesus do you think you might incorporate into your life? What would you have to sacrifice to do this?

Connecting With Scripture and Franciscan Writings—Third Letter of Saint John, Jude. *Clare: A Light in the Garden*, Murray Bodo, O.F.M.; or Piero Bargellini, *The Little Flowers of Saint Clare*; or *The Way of St. Francis*, Murray Bodo, O.F.M., pp. 25-31.

Application to Daily Life—Find a silent space to spend time each day with God alone. Perhaps a room at home with the phone off the hook, a corner in the town library on your lunch hour, a chapel, an empty workroom, a park bench can become your monastery for a time of contemplation. Use this time just to *listen* to God. Record in your journal what you experience. Encourage a friend or relative to seek silent time in which to listen to God. How might you *mirror* Clare in your home or workplace today?

Prayer—"O Saint Clare, your breadth and clarity of vision, your singleness of purpose and the shining example of your life make you a fitting patroness of television. We beg you to intercede for the leaders and all workers engaged in that important field, that television may become an influence for good upon all who view it, to the honor and glory of God. Oh, Saint Clare, to whom God revealed himself even on this earth, help us to see his Divine Wisdom in the marvelous development of science, so that we may use them in such wise ways as will lead us to the eternal vision of God, through Christ our Lord. Amen" (Leonard Foley, O.F.M., *Every Day and All Day*, pp. 111-112).

The Apostolates

An apostolate is the mission of an apostle. An apostle was one of the twelve disciples Jesus sent forth to carry his word and work throughout the world. If we choose to follow Jesus and to lead others to his truth, we become modern-day apostles. We have a mission, an apostolate. Apostolates are our special way of living Jesus' way of life. Perhaps you lead a Scripture study in your neighborhood or teach CCD to school children. You may work for reverence for all life in your community. Living a truly Christian life at your place of work may be your apostolate. Most Christians have several apostolates, though they may not call them that. Each way we help Jesus live in the world today becomes an apostolate.

The Secular Franciscan Order has Apostolic Commissions established to support the

apostolates of Work, Justice and Peace,
Ecology and Family within the fraternities.
Also of paramount importance in the
structure of the fraternity at all levels are
the Formation Commission and Youth
Commission. All of the apostolates help
bring Jesus' gifts of faith, hope and love
in tangible, practical ways. You will
discover these apostolates considered in
the following reflections.

Family Life:
Holiness in Its Place

"Happy those who endure in peace. By you, Most High, they will be crowned."

—Saint Francis, "The Canticle of the Creatures"

The life of God is not lived in a vacuum. We do not become Christians and then withdraw from relationships with others. Holiness is not something we find "outside" normal, everyday human activity. To be more precise, we do not join the Secular Franciscan Order to the detriment of any already-existing relationships. Wives who neglect their husbands or husbands who neglect their wives because they have "got religion" have the wrong idea of religion.

To be still more precise, any and all fruits of following Christ with Saint Francis must show up primarily in those relationships which are fundamental: family life. Charity and prayer, penance, poverty, humility—all must have their first fruits in what we contribute to the atmosphere of our home.

The Family, First and Vital Cell of Society

Sometimes we do not appreciate values simply because they are so valuable. Our civilization is built on the one man, one woman relationship of marriage. Our conventional wisdom, our traditions are taught and experienced there. Parents do not merely "produce" children. They set the tone of culture and religion. It is true that outside influences seem to be having a greater impact today than before TV made us all-knowing and cars and jets made us the most mobile creatures in history. But nothing can destroy the basic man-woman-children unit which God has made the foundation rock of society.

The Family: The Little Church

Equally obvious is the fact that there would be no "big Church" were it not for thousands of "little churches" where the Gospel takes root in the most intimate of personal relationships: man-wife, parent-child, brother-sister. The group of persons that comes together around the Eucharist is—or is trying to be—a community. They will succeed to the degree that they have given and forgiven, agonized and rejoiced in the little community from which they come.

Parents, First Teachers of the Faith

It is right that we value Catholic schools. They provide some experiences which the home cannot. They can organize the presentation of Catholic theory perhaps better than parents can. They can involve children in serving others on a broader scale but no teacher can replace a conscientious mother and father.

The meaning of the Christian life is best learned and best experienced from those with whom we have the deepest relationships. As the old saying has it, "The best thing a father can do for his children is love their mother."

Education

Vatican II confirms the role of the family: "Parents must be acknowledged as the *first and foremost educators of their children*. Their role as educators is so decisive that scarcely anything can compensate for their failure in it (Document on Education, No. 3).

The family is a kind of school of deeper humanity.... It needs the kindly communion of minds and the joint deliberation of the spouses, as well as the painstaking cooperation of parents in the education of their children. The active presence of the father is highly beneficial to their formation. The children, especially the younger ones, need the care of a mother at home. This domestic role of hers must be safely preserved, though the legitimate social progress of women should not be underrated on that account (Document on the Church Today, No. 52).

The above statement may cause argument among some. "But I must work! My kids need food on the table!" explains a young single mother. Certainly, some working mothers have no choice. Economic situations determine what they must do. In some families parents work out elaborate schedules so that their children are cared for by one parent or the other while the children are at home.

Yet the above statement is the view of the Church based on hundreds of years of experience of observing families. Children need parents to support and guide them as much as possible in their formative years. For some families this may mean sacrificing some of life's "extras." Maybe an extra TV or a pair of rollerblades must be a foregone pleasure. Supper might be cooked at home rather than purchased in a restaurant or ordered for carry-out. An affordable house or apartment rather than the tempting larger model for sale or rent reduces the financial burden a bit. "Extras" can come later. Children are important now.

Witnesses

Husbands and wives are witnesses of Christ's own mystery of love which he revealed to the world by his dying and rising to life again. When Christianity pervades a whole way of life, it gradually transforms it. In Christian homes husbands and wives find their proper vocation in being witnesses to one another and to their children of faith in Christ and love for him.

What Families Can Do

"Among the multiple activities of the family apostolate," says the *Document on the Laity*, "may be enumerated the following: the adoption of abandoned infants, hospitality to strangers, assistance in the operation of schools, helpful advice and material assistance for adolescents, help to engaged couples in preparing themselves for marriage, catechetical work, support of couples and families involved in material and moral crises, help for the aged."

Persons in the Single Vocation

Emphasis on the family as the bedrock of Church and state inevitably introduces a comparison of married and single persons. Persons leading a celibate life, and perhaps also living alone, have their own witness to give. They have benefited from family life and have made their contribution to their family. They may now be deeply involved in the various apostolic activities just mentioned. They do not share the particular satisfactions and problems of married life—a sacrifice on one hand, an advantage on the other. They may be more free to engage in the apostolic activities just mentioned. Their witness of a charitable, joyful and chaste life is rightly honored as an integral part of the Church's life and activity. The first two lay Franciscans were a married couple, Luchesio and Bona Donna. But as the secretary of Saint Bonaventure wrote, "The Third Order (Secular Franciscan Order) is equally for clerics and layfolk, maidens, widows and married people."

Questions for Reflection—What is the greatest gift parents have to give their children? In your own words describe the importance of family life to today's society.

Connecting With Scripture and Franciscan Writings—Creation, the fall, the promise of a redeemer in Genesis, Chapters 1-5. Bodo, pp. 94-99.

Application to Daily Life—As a parent, make a firm decision not to lose confidence in the normal processes of family life in the face of all other influences. As a single person, resolve to never underestimate the power of your witness. Pay attention to the influences within your home, always seeking to strengthen the family's choice to follow Christ. Choose one new activity this week to help bring your family closer to each other and to God.

Prayer—Thank you, Lord, for the blessings and the challenges of my family who help me become the special person I am created to be. Help me to forgive the hurts of family life and to rejoice in its miracles of love. Amen.

From the Rule of the Secular Franciscan Order

17. In their family they should cultivate the Franciscan spirit of peace, fidelity and respect for life, striving to make it a sign of a world already renewed in Christ.

   By living the grace of matrimony, husbands and wives in particular should bear witness in the world to the love of Christ for his Church. They should joyfully accompany their children on their human and spiritual journey by providing a simple and open Christian education and being attentive to the vocation of each child.

REFLECTION 32

Charity: Loving All People

"Wherever the friars meet one another, they should show that they are members of one family. And they should not hesitate to make known their needs to one another. For as a mother loves and cares for the child of her flesh, how much more should a friar love and care for his spiritual brother."
—*Saint Francis*, Rule of 1223, Chapter 6

To be God is to love. To share God's life, then, is to love like God, and indeed, to love like God made man. The essence of Christianity it to love God and neighbor and self *as Christ did* and by the power of his Spirit. No one knew this better than Francis of Assisi. His ideal was not merely to practice poverty, but to love the poor Christ and to be freed by the spirit of poverty from anything that might spoil his love of God and man.

What Is Love?

Since love is essential, it is also essential that we have a clear understanding of exactly what it is. The following definition is probably the most un-romantic one ever given, but it is a definition for all seasons: *Love is willing true goodness to someone.* Let's have a closer look at that meaning: a) *"Willing"*—a free and conscious act of our will, a decision that becomes an attitude. We say "willing" instead of "giving" because often we cannot give what we would like, such as health to a sick person, food to all the starving, relief to a disturbed person. But in any case it is our genuine willingness that counts; b) *"True goodness"*—not what we might selfishly want, not what they might mistakenly want, but what our best judgment of conscience tells us that God wants for them.

We see here that love can have degrees. Perfect love wills *all* that is good for someone. Perfect love is concerned with every need. Lesser love is *mainly* concerned with the genuine good of another but does not reach to all his needs. For example, a husband may love his wife very much and work hard for her support and comfort yet he may not be concerned enough for her emotional needs or for her spiritual needs.

We can love someone genuinely and at the same time want what they can do *for us*. Many people are so attractive that we just want to be with them—for the real pleasure they give us. We may work for a political candidate because we admire him and want him to succeed—realizing at the same time that we will benefit by his election. Obviously, when we are looking only for our own pleasure we can scarcely be said to love someone. c) *"For someone"*—ourselves or another. The great commandment says: "...and your neighbor as yourself," obviously implying that we are called to love ourselves.

Love of Self

In fact, we cannot love others genuinely if we do not love ourselves. Many people are under the terrible handicap of thinking themselves to be worthless. They have such a low opinion of themselves that they cannot believe that others really love them. And because they think that they are practically worthless, they do not feel that they have anything to give to others.

Most of us are fortunate enough to have good mothers and fathers who hovered over our cradle, cooed over us, cuddled us, thereby giving us the conviction that we were important little people. In the long process of maturing, we became whole persons by realizing that we are called to care for others just as our parents cared for us. Life is intended to be an ongoing process of "creation" whereby we all continue for each other what our parents started. We are called to be co-creators with God of ourselves and of each other. Sometimes loving another person into wholeness is a difficult process of healing when one has not had the experience of being created by others' love.

The Richness of Love

Love is complex. It is learned gradually and grows in ongoing personal relationships. Gradually we come to learn that this wonderful experience we receive from others and return in kind is an earthly sharing of God's own life. We learn that all real love has its power from God and is divine (never merely "natural") whether we realize it or not. Ultimately, we learn that God loved the world so much that he made his love visible in Jesus and showed us the absolute height of love in the voluntary death of Jesus on the cross.

The love of Jesus for himself, for all people and for God is the model and source of our own love. We really cannot love ourselves without realizing it is "normal" to go out of ourselves to love others. We cannot love others in a genuine way without being aware of God's presence in our love for each other. We cannot love God without wanting to share that relationship with others nor without realizing our own dignity.

Wherever there is genuine love, there is God. If a "heathen" man and woman love each other genuinely in the most remote wasteland or jungle, the Holy Spirit is creating that love and living in them—even if they have never heard of God or Jesus or the Spirit. All real love is God's love.

Christian Love

What, then, is distinctive about Christian love? It is a love that is *conscious* of the full extent of God's love made visible in Christ. Christian love is *aware* of all that God has said and done. It acts with the *realization* that the "love of God has been poured out in our hearts by the Holy Spirit, who is given to us." All that we do to others is done to Christ and for Christ. The only power to love that we possess is God's power in us. Christian love affirms that God has joined us together in his own family, has made us a member of his own divine community and in Jesus has shown us a perfect model of love in the most difficult of circumstances. A man or woman may love each other divinely without this knowledge—but it is far more difficult.

"Love is the reason for it all," says an old song. Love is at the center because it is the highest manifestation of the life of God. Love represents our own self-respect which can be maintained only by respecting others. Love is our gift to God returned by loving others.

Questions for Reflection—What is love? If it is real, is it "supernatural?" What are three elements of love?

Connecting With Scripture and Franciscan Writings—Noah and the ark in Genesis, Chapters 6-11. Bodo, pp. 99-101.

Application to Daily Life—Why do you love God? What do you love in your neighbor? Why do you love yourself? How have you shown love today? Examine the motives within your love for the person closest to you.

Prayer—Lord, I used to think charity meant giving away something and it does mean that. Thank you for enabling me to see that meaning in a new way: Charity means giving myself away in love to you and to others. Please keep me from being stingy in giving of myself. Amen.

From the Rule of the Secular Franciscan Order

12. Witnessing to the good yet to come and obliged to acquire purity of heart because of the vocation they have embraced, they should set themselves free to love God and their brothers and sisters.

The Forgiveness of Christ

"As surely as you love the Lord and me, see to it that no brother in the whole world, no matter how badly he has sinned, is ever allowed to go away from you without forgiveness, if he asks for it. And if he does not ask for forgiveness, then ask him if he does not want it. And if he comes a thousand times with sin, then love him altogether more than you love me, so that you may draw him to the Lord. And be always merciful to such persons."

—*Jorgenson*, Life of St. Francis

The Proof of Charity Is Forgiveness

We might as well get down to brass tacks right away—the test of our charity is the situation in which we are not loved: Someone does not apologize; someone continues to do something that irritates, exasperates, hurts or injures us. In that precise situation Christ says, "But I say to you, Love your enemies and pray for those who persecute you" (Matthew 5:44).

It is very easy to like and love good people. It may be relatively easy to forgive those who beg our pardon. It may not be a great sacrifice to forgive a great, dramatic injury. But the greatest test of our love of God and neighbor comes in those thousand daily incidents in which we do not get our way—when, in fact, someone else inflicts her will on us.

No Self-defense?

Forgiveness must accompany the just pursuit of our rights. We may be forced to speak up when there is a question of injustice to ourselves or others. We may have to call the police, sue, go to higher authority, argue, persist. None of these things is incompatible with forgiveness. Forgiveness loves another person no matter what he has done or what we have to do.

If We Have God's Life, We Must Act Like God

We inevitably think of God in our own image. So we think of God as being "mad" at us for something we did. Then we repent and God gets over his "mad" and forgives us. The fact is, of course, that God's love never changes. His love does not depend on our virtue (though our happiness does). God's forgiveness simply means that he keeps on loving us as he always did. God's love takes the *form* of the sign-sacrament of reconciliation and the assurance of good friends. In this form it looks like a new development. But God has not changed.

Since our God is that way and we have that divine life, we have no choice but to act the same way. We have the privilege of being like God. Note that the *reason* Jesus gave for forgiving our enemies is that, "you may be children of your Father in heaven; for he makes his sun rise on the evil and on the good, and sends rain on the righteous and on the unrighteous" (Matthew 5:44). If being like God isn't enough reason to forgive, there is no reason good enough.

Sinful Anger Is Revenge

Most people would not think of themselves as particularly vengeful. Yet all sinful anger is nothing but giving in to the desire for revenge. If our pride is hurt by what seems like contempt in others—even those who love us—we feel we must strike back, hurt them, to prove that we have power, too.

On the other hand, justifiable anger attacks evil, not persons. Such anger is moderate and good-intentioned. We cannot imagine Christ striking others with whips in the Temple simply out of hurt pride, revenge, exasperation or loss of temper. Our Lord simply did what he had to do for his Father's honor. But he loved these same hypocrites, adulterers and murderers enough to die for them. And we his followers can do no less.

There may be times when it is only prudent to prefer one person over another, actively to oppose someone's being appointed to office, to administer correction, even to punish. The only test as to whether the anger is charitable or not is this: *Am I really trying to do good to this person as Christ would?*

No matter what anyone has done to us, we can and must wish him the blessing of God. We do not have to go out of our way in displaying affection. But we must give this person the civilities that all good people would expect us to give even in these circumstances.

Forgiveness does not mean liking *what* another does. On the other hand, the saying, "I love you, but I do not like you" seems to contain the seeds of failure within it. If we love someone, we can at least try to find something to like.

125

We Need God's Forgiveness

In offending one another, not loving one another, we do *not* do God's will; we "offend God." Only God can forgive sin. We who receive God's forgiveness are to forgive one another. "Forgive as the Lord has forgiven you" (Colossians 3:13).

To Free Ourselves

One of the beautiful incidents in Saint Francis's life centered around forgiveness. Francis found a man bitterly cursing the employer who had cheated him—literally wishing that God would damn him. Francis begged him to find forgiveness in his heart so that the man *could free himself.* We cannot be free, peaceful children of God if we nourish a vindictive attitude in our heart.

Questions for Reflection—What is the acid test of true charity? Why should you forgive your neighbor? What does it mean to forgive? When is anger sinful? What is the most practical reason for forgiving others?

Connecting With Scripture and Franciscan Readings—Abraham, father of the chosen people, in Genesis, Chapters 12-17. Bodo, pp. 101-103.

Application to Daily Life—How can you best go about forgiving the person who irritates you the most? Can you justify the way you oppose others? How much of your anger is reasonable and Christlike? Are you over-strict or over-demanding with others? Are you able to pass over other's faults in silence? As you pray the Our Father, think of the mercy available to you by forgiving others.

Prayer—"Forgive us our trespasses as we forgive those who trespass against us." You did that, Jesus. Help me to forgive as you did. Amen.

REFLECTION 34

Being Christ to Others

"In Saint Francis's later life, a leper occasioned another beautiful example of his charity and its Christlike power.

"The leper complained that the Brothers did not take care of him properly. Francis simply said, 'Shall I take care of you?' The leper answered, 'I would like that.' Francis said, 'I will do all you wish.' The leper, 'Then I want you to wash me all over, the odor is so bad, I cannot stand it.'

"Then Francis took warm water and aromatic herbs, undressed the sick man and began to wash him. As he touched the leper's body with his hands, the leprosy began to be cured. And the man's soul began to be cured also. The leper began to cry, first softly, then aloud. 'I am worthy of hell for the injustice I have done the Brothers, and for my impatience and blasphemy.' But Francis thanked God for so great a miracle and hurried away, lest honor come to him."

—Jorgensen, Life of St. Francis

Being and Seeing

The practice of charity can be summed up in two phrases:

1) Being Christ to others and seeing Christ in others;

2) Loving others as Christ loves them and loving Christ in others.

Almost everybody has asked the question, at least in his heart, "How can I possibly see Christ in *him*? in *her*?" Perhaps we will find the answer by first taking care of *being* Christ to others. We may then find him very easily in those we serve.

Christ "Needs" Us

We, the Body of Christ, continue the life and work of Christ on earth today. If the world is to know how Christ loves, heals, forgives, it must have visible examples in the members of the Church.

Now, the essence of the life of Christ is that he simply "went about doing good." He continues that activity today. The Head needs the hands, even ours, to bless and heal and wash the wounds of others.

What Are We Called to Do?

To speak to others, offering understanding, encouragement, cheerfulness, patience, peace;

To help them carry their burdens and believe that God loves them (we are the evidence!);

To be open to their needs and to respect their privacy;

To admire and support their physical, emotional or spiritual suffering;

To give them food, clothing, shelter;

To support them in their fight for human rights, for a decent opportunity to grow as human beings and children of God;

To suffer with them and for them, in Christ;

To work for their salvation by prayer and penance.

The Power to Act Like God

We are called to be Christ, the loving Child of the Father, the Brother of all his fellow human beings. We have been made adopted children of the Father possessing God's own life. The most obvious result is that we are to act like God, as every child acts like its father and mother. To be a Christian is to love as God loves or as Christ loves—which is the same thing. When God gave us his life, we received in the universe, the *power to love like God*. This is not merely imitating externally what Christ did on earth. We have an inner reality, the life of God living within our freedom, whereby we love as God loves, with his power, joy and fruitfulness.

The Chivalrous Saint

Saint Francis had a great love for his mother's land, France, and for its tales of knightly glory and courtly love. After his conversion, the delicate courtesy and respect for every person remained. Francis's charity was not only dramatic and heroic and exercised on a broad scale in the Church. It extended to the minor dramas of everyday life where most of us tend to be "off duty."

Perhaps the most precious story about the courtesy of Francis has to do with the midnight snack at Rivo Torto. At that dark and desolate hour, a voice was heard in the crowded little dormitory. "Oh, I am dying, I am dying!" Francis and the other friars awakened and struck a light. Francis asked, and we can see him smiling, "Who is dying?" One of the friars confessed that he was dying of hunger. Instead of dressing the man down as a weakling among giants in asceticism, Francis gently suggested that they all have a snack. It probably wasn't pizza and beer—more like carrots and water—but it was a simple, delightful party and recognized human weakness and made the least of it.

Being Christ is not only giving one's life on the cross. It is ordering food for a little girl just raised from the dead, asking for a drink of water because the Samaritan woman needed his healing, being concerned about the embarrassment of a bride and groom at Cana and putting his arms around the little children.

Questions for Reflection—How can you continue the charity of Christ? What authority do you have for saying that Christ needs you?

Connecting With Scripture and Franciscan Writings—Isaac, son of Abraham, in Genesis, Chapters 18-23. Bodo, pp. 103-105.

Application to Daily Life—How can you be Christ in your own home? on the street? at work? at a dance? Ask yourself as often as possible: What would Christ do right now? What does Christ wish you to do, and to do in you, right now?

Prayer—Lord Jesus, it has been said that you have no hands for your work and caring on earth today except our hands. Please use mine. Amen.

From the Rule of the Secular Franciscan Order

14. Secular Franciscans, together with all people of good will, are called to build a more fraternal and evangelical world so that the kingdom of God may be brought about more effectively. Mindful that anyone "who follows Christ, the perfect man, becomes more of a man himself," let them exercise their responsibilities competently in the Christian spirit of service.

Seeing Christ in Others

"Whoever comes to them, friend or foe, thief or robber, let him be received with kindness...They must rejoice when they live among people considered of little value and looked down upon, among the poor and the powerless, the sick and the lepers, and the beggars by the wayside."

—*Saint Francis*, Earlier Rule

Can We Really See Christ in Others?

Obviously we cannot see Christ in someone's rage, selfishness, laziness, cruelty or stubbornness. And since most of us have at least a smidgen of all of these, isn't this ideal of seeing Christ in others just that—an ideal, and a rather distant one at that?

We are sure, theoretically, that it is not an impossible ideal, but it remains the difficult virtue of the Christian life since it involves faith, forgiveness and a refusal to judge others.

True love is not divisible. Genuine love of God implies love of neighbor and self. Genuine love of neighbor and self can come only out of a love of God. So far, so good.

What we can see in my vindictive, inconsiderate, domineering neighbor (and in our own non-spotless selves) is a "live" image of God. We see a total person whom God loves as he is because that person, beneath the sin and ugliness, mirrors at least some of the attributes of God: He is free, intelligent, *capable* of the highest love. Even if that freedom has been enslaved or that intelligence is clouded by physical, emotional or moral obstacles, that person is *at least* like the song that waits to be released from the throat of a sleeping singer.

We must never get the notion that God patronizes us, treats us as if we were worth loving when everyone knows that we're not. God does not pretend or do things half-heartedly or "officially." *He takes every one of us seriously.*

Human and Divine

We can say that Christ "added" new dignity to human nature by the union of the divine and the human. In the one person of Christ, human nature is inseparably and forever united to God.

But perhaps it is equally important to say that Christ did not "add" anything to human nature. Rather he made visible the love that had never changed. The first human beings were already loved with this love and the theology of Duns Scotus holds that from eternity Christ was destined to be the head and center of the human race. The only reason for this is: God is love.

Every human being, therefore, is an immeasurably valuable friend of God, clothed in the love of God and marked with the most perfect visible sign of God's love—a human nature like that of the head of the human race.

We are the "unfinished" children of God. God is working hard on us. God, of course, has no difficulty in seeing the end-product he has in mind—unique human beings, each as individual as their fingerprints—and each bearing his or her family likeness to the firstborn Son.

We are not playing games when we speak of "seeing" Christ in others. In fact, it is only when we *are* playing games that "seeing Christ in others" can be meaningless pretense.

The Example of Francis

Some of the most charming stories about Saint Francis spring out of his very real vision of Christ in others. He seems always to be giving away his cloak with a very vivid sense of giving it to Christ. Once, for instance, he heard of a poor woman who could not pay the expenses of medical treatment for her eyes. He called one of the brothers who was his Superior and said, "Brother Guardian, we have to pay back a loan." "What is the loan, Brother?" Francis answered, "This cape which we have borrowed from that poor sick woman. We must give it back to her." Wondering at Saint Francis's faith the Superior said, "Brother, do as you think best." Then Francis, most pleased, called one of his friends and said: "Take this cloak and a dozen loaves of bread. Go to that poor woman and say to her, 'The poor man to whom you loaned this cloak thanks you for the loan. Take what is yours.'" The woman was at first suspicious, then surprised, then overjoyed. But she was careful to leave in the dead of night, lest this peculiar man change his mind (Jorgensen, *Life of St. Francis*).

God's Intention

God's intention is that every person we meet be with us someday in heaven, purified and glorious, with intelligence balanced and brilliant, with love made Christlike and with a body radiant and perfect. We must see this now. For this will be our judgment: "I was hungry (for kindness) and you gave it. I was thirsty (for patience) and you gave it. I was sick (with sin) and you took care of me. I was in the prison (of my own selfishness) and you helped me break the chains."

Questions for Reflection—Why does God love every human being? Did Christ "add" anything to human nature? What is God's plan for everyone?

Connecting With Scripture and Franciscan Writings—Jacob, father of the twelve tribes of Israel, in Genesis, Chapters 25-29. Bodo, pp. 106-107.

Application to Daily Life—What does God see of Christ in you? Why are you lovable? Is this same quality present in everyone you meet? Make a deliberate effort to see Christ, attractive or deformed, in one definite person.

Prayer—Teach me, Lord, to look deeply into others to find you there. It's so easy to focus on the "unfinished" part of a person and miss your Spirit that might be veiled behind a grumpy face, an angry word, a proud expression. Give me the eyes of your Spirit to see as you see. Amen.

From the Rule of the Secular Franciscan Order

13. As the Father sees in every person the features of his Son, the firstborn of many brothers and sisters, so the Secular Franciscans, with a gentle and courteous spirit, accept all people as a gift of the Lord and an image of Christ.

   A sense of community will make them joyful and ready to place themselves on an equal basis with all people, especially with the lowly for whom they shall strive to create conditions of life worthy of people redeemed by Christ.

REFLECTION 36

Justice: The First Requirement of Charity

"Let no one imagine that there is any opposition between these two things: the perfection of one's own soul and the business of this life, as if one had no chance but to abandon the activities of this world in order to strive for Christian perfection.... When one is motivated by Christian charity, he cannot but love others and regard the needs, sufferings and joys of others as his own."

—*Pope John XXIII,* Mater et Magistra

Justice and Charity

We can make two serious errors about justice and charity. First, we can think that justice concerns what we *must* do for others and charity is what we *may* do for them—a sort of bonus virtue. Second, we can put justice in the category of *things*—pay the money you owe—and charity in the area of *persons*—love your neighbor.

This unfortunate divorce has led to monstrous consequences. It enabled us to be very "honest"—we couldn't think of stealing a dime—and yet quite unconcerned about the fact that many of our brothers and sisters live in a state of perpetual deprivation of the most basic rights. We have somehow felt that it was charitable to send them band-aid donations of food and old clothing. We didn't really owe them anything in the way that we owed the banker or the milkman. In short, we could somehow be just yet unloving, or loving but unjust.

Justice is impossible without love. Love is absolute and irreplaceable. All other virtues and practices must be expressions of it. If justice is to be a Christian value, it must be a justice of love or it is no justice at all. It is important—as just love or loving justice—to pay debts and fulfill contracts. But there is an urgent need to be concerned about justice on a more basic level, particularly with a concern for the poor, the deprived, the unemployed, the uneducated, the handicapped. The greatest injustice is perpetuated by institutions, the complex systems

133

humans devise to fulfill their purposes. Injustice can be built into the very culture and social customs of a nation.

Discriminative housing patterns are supported by people who "want only what is best for their children" and who want to "maintain quality education." Deceit in government is approved by all who realize that "you have to cut a few corners to get someplace." Trade agreements keep developing countries in a state of poverty because we must keep our own economy healthy.

The Example of Saint Francis

Most people would not immediately think of Saint Francis as a social reformer, yet the Third Order (S.F.O.) itself was a great instrument of reform. No lay Franciscan was allowed to bear arms to be used against any person. This was a deadly blow against a system of enforced military service whereby petty feudal lords could force their subjects into fighting their wars of conquest and revenge. At Faenza, for instance, many of the citizens had joined the Penitential Brothers, as the Third Order (S.F.O.) was then called. When the mayor wished them to take the usual oath of obedience whereby they would oblige themselves to take up arms when the authorities ordered it, they refused to swear (shades of our modern conscientious objectors!) under the claim that to swear such an oath involved taking up arms, and that was against their Rule. The mayor tried to force the Brotherhood to take the oath. Apparently they turned in their need to Francis' friend, Cardinal Hugolino. The Pope then ordered the bishop to take the Penitential Brothers under his protection. This dispute soon spread all over Italy. As a sort of punishment the cities subjected the Penitential Brothers to special taxes and forbade their giving their property to the poor. In a circular letter to all Italian bishops, the Pope ordered all the clergy to take the side of the Brothers against the public authorities. And so the Third Order (S.F.O.) brought about at least a partial disarming of the quarrelsome Italian republics (Jorgensen, *Life of St. Francis*).

Today's Problems

Secular Franciscans today may not have such a clear-cut choice as taking or rejecting a military oath. But the fact that our problems are complex and emotional is no excuse for avoiding them. One of these, almost certainly the worst, is the problem of racism. This is a moral problem, not an educational, economic or political one. It has to do with persons, children of God. It should go without saying that a Christian is concerned about the material and spiritual welfare of his brothers and sisters. Most Christians believe they are actually concerned and unprejudiced. Yet they may continue to use derogatory names for people of other ethnic groups, treasure stories about what "they" do, thus perpetuating a scandal to the Church.

The Gospel

Justice is a matter of taking charity seriously. If we are with the Church as Francis was, then we will be challenged by the clear call to action given by Pope Paul and the bishops at the 1971 Synod: "Action on behalf of justice and participation in the transformation of the world fully appear to us as a *constitutive* dimension of the preaching of the Gospel." In other words, action for justice is one of the elements that *constitutes* the proclamation of the Good News. If it is missing, the gospel is crippled.

Questions for Reflection—Can there be justice without charity? Can there be charity without justice? Name two errors in this regard.

Connecting With Scripture and Franciscan Writing—Joseph, savior of his brothers, in Genesis, Chapters 37-50. Bodo, pp. 108-110.

Application to Daily Life—What do you think is the greatest injustice in your state? county? city? neighborhood? In your own way of looking at life? Try to examine your language and conversation for unrealized expressions of prejudice.

Prayer—I ask you, Lord, for a heart that loves enough to want the best for all people. Amen.

From the Rule of the Secular Franciscan Order

15. Let them individually and collectively be in the forefront in promoting justice by the testimony of their human lives and their courageous initiatives. Especially in the field of public life, they should make definite choices in harmony with their faith.

REFLECTION 37

Justice: Bringing the Gospel to the World

"The faithful, and more precisely the laity, are stationed in the front ranks of the Church, and through them the Church is the living principle of human society. Consequently, they especially must have an ever increasing consciousness, not only of belonging to the Church, but of being the Church."

—Pope Pius XII

The Justice and Peace Apostolate

Many people would like to do good, to be apostles, to help society, but they don't know where to begin. What is a layperson supposed to do, anyway?

First, let us see the general problem. The popes in their encyclicals tell us that we have a double duty. We must try to produce a morally better society and we must try to produce a society whose institutions are better.

Social Institutions

The word "institution" needs explaining. It simply means the big, organized ways by which society takes care of its needs, keeps the wheels of civilization moving ahead. Certain basic needs of humankind have always been present. They may have been taken care of in different ways, but the basic needs are the same:

Political: We need (and adopt) some kind of governing organizations;

Economic: We need (and adopt) some method of producing and distributing goods;

Educational: We need (and adopt) some method of training and teaching the young;

Family: We need (and have) a system of family life to continue the race;

136

Recreational: We need (and have) a general way of diversion and play;

Religious: We must worship God as a society.

The Influence of Institutions

What the Australian Bishops said years ago seems to hold true today. A "prime cause of the mass suffering of people" is that they are "dominated by organized bodies whose policies are dictated by men acting in defiance of the moral law. Sin has been elevated to the level of policy in certain organizations whose acts dominate the lives of entire communities. And the wages of mass sin is mass death."

The popes have been most solicitous about these institutions that have so great an influence on us. We must not deal in strictly "spiritual" things. We must try to Christianize the six institutions mentioned above. Cardinal Suhard of France stated: "The layman may no longer content himself with sanctifying individual lives; he owes it to himself to Christianize 'social institutions' such as his neighborhood, his class, leisure activities, the movies, radio...."

Reforming Institutions

Someone may say, "Society is made up of individuals. So, convert the individuals and society will automatically be converted." But it doesn't work exactly that way. Institutions themselves are too powerful. For instance, individuals may want to improve working conditions and wages in a highly competitive industry. If they do it alone, however, they may go bankrupt. They will have to work toward getting employers together to better the whole economic institution. A parent does not want children subjected to the objectionable magazines at the corner drugstore. Working alone, the parent may not be able to accomplish as much as by joining with other parents to influence publishers and distributors.

The social apostolate will almost always have to be organized in order to carry our personal apostolates into society. A few people will be in positions to influence society directly: those who hold important positions in government, business, unions, community organizations. Most people can help only indirectly. Perhaps the greatest need today is education in the social teachings of the Church. Many a good movement dies because people are not interested. They are not interested because they do not know anything about these topics.

However, while the unity of a group endeavor may carry greater influence in reforming institutions, we must never forget that most group activities begin with the discernment of need, the vision and the energy of an individual. As individuals we must never feel we are powerless when we act for justice.

A Specific Example of the Social Apostolate

To summarize, let us take as an example a young, educated couple, married with preschool-age children. For them the lay apostolate has three facets:

> *First*, there is the personal apostolate of prayer and good example. Every Catholic can and must do this, no matter what else he or she cannot do.

> *Second*, this husband and wife must Christianize their own family life. This must come before all other work. Perhaps they may belong to a group which will help them do this themselves and likewise help other families. The Christian Family Movement (CFM) is an excellent organization for this purpose.

> *Finally*, the couple may work to bring Christ into the society in which they live. Depending on the time the couple has available after taking care of their primary family and work duties, and depending on their talents and training, the couple may take part an organization for political or social improvement.

In any case, he or she is not concerned only with saving his or her own soul; each is concerned with saving the souls of others. They are not concerned only with their own worldly well-being, rights and privileges; they are concerned about the rights and well-being of *all* human beings. It is a huge, complex task which will take a lifetime. But we must do what we can while we can. We must learn what the problems are, look for opportunities to help, join with others in organizations to "reform the institutions." (Material for this lesson was taken from *The Emerging Layman* by Donald Thorman.)

Questions for Reflection—What is our double duty? What are the "institutions" of society? Why is the Christianization of individuals not enough? What may be the Catholic's greatest social need? What is a person's first obligation? What is a husband's or wife's first obligation?

Connecting With Scripture and Franciscan Writings—Moses, leader of the chosen people, in Exodus, Chapters 1-5. Bodo, pp. 110-112.

Application to Daily Life—Do you recall being greatly interested in working for justice in your community? In working for an adequate family wage for all people? Have you skipped voting for no good reason? Which of the six institutions could you possibly affect directly? Which one can you attempt to Christianize indirectly? Can we ignore any of them? Examine your conscience to discover whether you have been selfish in regard to your obligation to society.

Prayer—Each of your saints, Lord, possesses the quality of courage. Fill me with your strength of heart, called courage, to live the gospel in a world that too often denies that you are Lord. Amen.

Justice: Our New Social Problems

*"....Where there is hatred, let me sow love,
where there is injury, pardon."*

—*Saint Francis, "The Peace Prayer"*

Seeking Justice

Pope Paul VI issued an Apostolic Letter, "A Call to Action," on the eightieth anniversary of Pope Leo's great encyclical, *Rerum Novarum*. More recently Pope John Paul II again called attention to the century-old document, stating that its "teaching is not limited to protest, but throws a far-seeing glance toward the future" (*Crossing the Threshold of Hope*, p. 131). Pope Paul spelled out new areas which Christian social justice must consider. This chapter touches upon some of the issues which most concerned him, summarizing his words in some instances.

"Today," he said, "the social question has become worldwide. A renewed consciousness of the demands of the Gospel makes it the Church's duty to put herself at the service of all.... Solidarity in action at *this turning point in history* is an urgent matter.... These (following) questions must in the years to come take first place among the preoccupations of Christians, because of their urgency, extent and complexity."

Urbanization

Our former agricultural civilization is weakening. This flight from the land, plus industrial growth, population expansion and the attraction of big cities brings about great concentrations of population—sometimes millions. Meanwhile, industrialization allows certain businesses to develop while others die or move. Thus, new social problems are created: professional or regional unemployment, the movement of workers, the elimination of some jobs and creation of others by changes in technology, uneven conditions in various branches of industry. Unlimited competition with modern advertising methods and e-commerce via the

Internet incessantly launches new products and tries to attract new consumers while other industrial plants, still capable of functioning, become useless. Large areas of the population cannot satisfy their primary needs while superfluous needs are cleverly created. So the penetrating question must be asked: Having controlled nature, is man now becoming the slave of the things he makes?

Christians in the City

In an industrial society, urbanization can upset the family, the neighborhood and the very framework of the Christian community. Man is experiencing a new loneliness in an anonymous crowd which surrounds him, in which he feels himself a stranger.

New working classes are born in the heart of the cities sometimes abandoned by the rich. They form a belt of misery, a silent protest against the luxury, consumption and waste they see so near to them. The big city can foster discrimination and indifference. It lends itself to new forms of exploitation and domination. Misery spreads where human dignity flounders amid delinquency, violence, criminality, abuse of drugs and sex.

There is an urgent need to reweave the social fabric so that humans can develop and improve themselves and their conditions, while still providing for their needs. Cultural centers must be created or developed at the community or parish levels. Christians must discover new modes of neighborliness, apply social justice in an original manner and take responsibility for our common future.

Youth

There have always been pitfalls and difficulties in communication between generations. Mistakes in this area can sometimes produce serious conflict, even within families. Our task as Christians is to respect the energy, aspirations and challenge of our youth while handing on the values upon which our society and religion depend.

The Role of Women

There is lively demand for an end to discrimination of women and to establish equal rights. In pursuing these aims, we must take care to prevent a false equality that would deny women the opportunity to choose to fulfill their historical roles at the heart of the family and of society. Legislation and our Christian attitude should protect women, their independence as individuals and their equal rights to participate in cultural, economic, political and social life.

Workers

Every individual has a right to work, to develop qualities and personality in the exercise of a profession and to receive a just wage which will enable families to lead a worthy life on the material, social, cultural and spiritual level. Workers must have the right to provide for medical insurance and for assistance with needs arising from advancing years.

The important role of union organizations must be recognized—the representation of workers, working together for economic advancement of society and a responsibility for the common good. But the temptation arises to impose, especially by strikes, conditions which may be detrimental to the overall economy and society.

We must never forget that the purpose of work at our jobs is to use our God-given talents and *to make a living, not to make a killing*. With this in mind we will remember that *just* wages mean fair wages for workers at both ends of the salary scale, not colossal paychecks and tremendous perks at one end of the scale and meager, subsistence-level pay at the other end.

Franciscans affirm the position of Jesus and Francis that individuals have worth not because of what they can produce but because of who they are in the eyes of God.

Victims of Change

Discernment is needed to strike at the roots of new situations of injustice. In an industrial society with its constant and rapid change, more and more people are personally disadvantaged. The Church directs her attention to these new "poor"—the disabled and mentally challenged, older people, various minority groups, the working poor—in order to recognize them, help them, and defend their place and dignity in a society hardened by competition.

The rights of workers to maintain benefits of health care and retirement benefits must be protected, particularly when corporate downsizing and restructuring create job losses.

Discrimination

Among victims of injustice must be placed those who are discriminated against because of their race, ethnic origin, culture, sex, sexual orientation or religion.

Racial and ethnic discrimination is an injustice particularly important in our times, creating tension around the world. All members of the human race share the same basic rights and duties and the same eternal destiny. All should be equal before the law, find equal admittance to economic, cultural civic and social life and should benefit from a fair sharing of the nation's riches and opportunities.

Immigrant Workers

Many immigrant workers have difficulty in becoming socially established in their adopted country even though they provide it with essential labor. These workers should be integrated and provision made for their personal and professional advancement, and access to decent housing where their families can join them.

Everyone, and especially Christians, must work for universal brotherhood. We cannot in truthfulness call upon that God who is the Parent of all if we refuse to act in a brotherly way toward certain men and women created in God's image.

The Media

The media have greatly influenced the quantity and quality of information we receive, transforming our society. Those in the media have a serious moral responsibility to the truth, to the needs and reactions they generate and the values they put forward. We all have a serious moral responsibility to keep the media mindful of their role and to act to ensure that that responsibility is upheld.

The Environment

We are suddenly becoming aware that our exploitation of nature carries grave risks to health and life for ourselves and our entire planet. We must be aware of how our everyday choices can contribute to the destruction of the environment. Do we waste the energy of which our society is a disproportionate consumer? Do we reduce our consumption, reuse what we can and recycle as much as possible? Do we seek ways to simplify our life-styles that will help produce a healthier environment?

A Call to Action

"Laymen should take up as their proper task the renewal of the temporal order...take the initiative freely and infuse a Christian spirit into the mentality, customs, laws and structures of the community in which they live. Words are useless without a lively awareness of personal responsibility and effective action. The Christian hope comes primarily from the fact that he knows that the Lord is working with us in the world."

"Be not afraid," Jesus said to his followers (Luke 24:36). John Paul II chose those words to begin his pontificate. They echo to us today. We must not be afraid to go forth to do what Jesus would do to create a better world beginning with the place we live.

Questions for Reflection—What basic Christian principles are involved in the discussion of these problems? Does the Church—and do individual Christians—bear responsibility to help solve them?

Connecting With Scripture and Franciscan Writings—The plagues, the paschal lamb in Exodus, Chapters 6-12. Bodo, pp. 112-114.

Application to Daily Life—What concrete examples of injustice suffered by the poor can you think of? Choose one situation and decide on one simple thing you can do to bring justice. Decide on a practical way in which you can simplify your way of living and help the environment.

Prayer—Creator God, you commanded your creation to be fertile and multiply and we did. We are many and so often we can't get along with one another. Families split, citizens argue and fight, countries war. In the midst of conflict, help us to live your solution to our social problems: "Love one another as I have loved you." Amen.

REFLECTION 39

The Practice of Justice

"And every member is to give the treasurer one ordinary denar. The treasurer is to collect this money and distribute it on the advice of the ministers among the poor brothers and sisters, especially the sick and those who may have nothing for their funeral services; and thereupon among other poor; and they are to offer something of the money to the church."

—*Saint Francis*, First Rule of the Third Order, 1221

The Church's Witness

One of the important documents in the Church's tradition on social justice is "Justice in the World," issued by the Synod of Bishops called by Pope Paul in 1971. This lesson is a summary of the third chapter of that document, entitled "The Practice of Justice."

The Church recognizes that those who venture to speak to people about justice must first be just themselves. Hence we must first examine the life-style found within the Church herself, our ways of acting, our material possessions.

Rights must be preserved within the Church for those who serve her. Those who are associated with the Church, laity, men and women, should receive a sufficient livelihood via fair wages and a system for promotion to enjoy the social security that is customary in their region. Progress has been made in the laity exercising more important functions with regard to Church property and sharing in its administration.

Freedom of Expression and Thought: The Church recognizes everyone's right to suitable freedom of expression and thought. This includes the right of everyone to be heard in a spirit of dialogue that preserves legitimate diversity within the Church.

Judicial Procedure: The accused has a right to know his accusers and also the right to a proper defense. To be complete, justice should include speed in procedure. This is especially true in marriage cases.

Shared Responsibility: In accordance with the rules drawn up by Vatican II and the Holy See, the members of the Church should have some share in the drawing up of decisions. Laity should take an active role in councils at all levels of Church which deal with concerns of all the members of the Church.

Earthly Goods: It must never happen that the Gospel witness of the Church be clouded by the material riches we possess no matter how we use them. The same must be said about the privileges the Church has. Our faith demands of us a certain sparingness in the use of things. We should live and administer our goods in such a way that the Good News is convincingly proclaimed to the poor. If the Church appears to be identified with the rich and powerful of the world, its credibility is diminished or lost.

Life-style: Bishops, priests, religious, laity—all must examine their life-styles. Does belonging to the Church put us on a rich island in the midst of poverty? In our affluent society, does our life-style give an example of that sparingness in consumption which we claim to be necessary in order to feed millions of hungry people in the world?

Education for Justice

Education for justice is imparted first in the family, also in the work-place, schools, the Church. The content of this education necessarily involves respect for the person and his dignity. First of all, the unity of the human family is to be emphasized. All human beings are destined to become, in Christ, sharers in the divine nature.

The basic principles whereby the gospel life can make itself felt in contemporary social life are to be found in the body of teaching set forth in the documents of Vatican II and in the social encyclicals: "*Gaudium et Spes*: Pastoral Constitution on the Church in the Modern World"; "*Apostolicam Actuositatem*: Decree on the Apostolate of the Laity"; "*Laborem Exercens*: On Human Work"; "*Christifidelis Laici*: The Vocation and Mission of the Lay Faithful in the Church and the World"; "The Condition of Labor," Pope Leo XIII; "Reconstructing the Social Order," Pope Pius XI; "Christianity and Social Progress and Peace on Earth," Pope John XXIII; "Development of Peoples and Call to Action," Pope Paul VI; "The Church in the Modern World," Vatican II; "Justice in the World," 1971 Synod document.

(See the Resources section for further information on these docu-ments.)

Welcome or unwelcome, the Word of God should be present in the center of human situations. Our statements should always be in harmony with the circumstances of place and time and be a true expression of the faith. Our mission also demands that we denounce injustice, with charity, prudence and firmness and in sincere dialogue with all parties concerned.

Finally, the liturgy can greatly serve education for justice, helping us discover the teaching of the prophets and the Lord and the apostles on the subject of justice. Preparation for Baptism is the beginning of the formation of the Christian conscience. The practice of Reconciliation should emphasize the social dimension of sin and of the sacrament. The Eucharist forms the community and places it at the service of humankind.

Cooperation of Churches

Great cooperation should exist between the local Catholic churches of rich and poor regions, both through spiritual communion and by a sharing of human and material resources. We Catholics should also cooperate with other Christian brethren to promote human dignity and fundamental human rights, especially the right to religious liberty. We can make a common effort against discrimination based on religion, race, culture or sex. Collaboration extends also to the study of the gospel teachings as the inspiration for all Christian activity. We should, indeed, cooperate with all believers in God in the fostering of social justice, peace and freedom.

International Action

The international order is rooted in the inalienable rights and dignity of the human being. The United Nations Declaration of Human Rights should be observed by all. The United Nations; Franciscans International, a non-governmental organization of the United Nations; and other international organizations should be supported insofar as they are the beginning of a system striving to restrain the armed hostilities between nations and settling conflicts by peaceful methods.

Attention should be given the bishops' position on social justice issues. These include studying the pardon of debt of third-world countries, fairer prices for raw materials, the opening of the markets of the richer nations and protection of human rights in the workplaces of all nations.

A World of Hope

The power of the Spirit is continuously at work in the world. The people of God are present among the poor and those who suffer persecution and oppression. The Body of Christ, the Church, lives in its own flesh the passion of Christ and bears witness to all people of his Resurrection.

The radical transformation of the world in the paschal mystery gives full meaning to the efforts of people to lessen injustice, violence and hatred and to advance together in justice, freedom, brotherhood and love.

Questions for Reflection—How can the Secular Franciscan Order cooperate with the stated aims of the Church's teaching on social justice? How can the local fraternity work toward these aims?

Connecting With Scripture and Franciscan Writings—The chosen people in the desert, manna and water, in Exodus, Chapters 13-18. Bodo, pp. 115-116.

Application to Daily Living—Which of the points under "The Church's Witness" is most meaningful to you? Have you read any of the documents mentioned? Seriously consider learning about or cooperating in some project to promote justice and peace.

Prayer—Lord, to truly practice justice in your world I must see circumstances from not just my point of view but from the perspective of others—the poor, the uneducated, the imprisoned, the persecuted. Please, Lord, give me a broader vision of your world and the courage to become an instrument of change. Amen.

From the Rule of the Secular Franciscan Order

6. They have been made living members of the Church by being buried and raised with Christ in baptism; they have been united more intimately with the Church by profession. Therefore, they should go forth as witnesses and instruments of her mission among all people, proclaiming Christ by their life and words.

Called like Saint Francis to rebuild the Church and inspired by his example, let them devote themselves energetically to living in full communion with the pope, bishops, and priests, fostering an open and trusting dialogue of apostolic effectiveness and creativity.

The Apostolate of Peacemaking

"The Lord revealed to me a salutation, that we should say: 'The Lord give you peace'."

—Saint Francis, The Testament

Francis and Peace

Francis of Assisi was an extremely simple man who understood the very heart of life. We know that the desire for peace is one of the deepest desires of the heart of man—and of Christ. Wherever Francis went, he would greet people with, "The Lord give you peace!" And he meant it!

Blessed Are the Peacemakers

Saint Francis lived the beatitudes of our Lord. "Blessed are the poor in spirit" was the wellspring of his sanctity. "Blessed are the peacemakers" was the light of his apostolate. Because these words were in the Gospel, he wanted them to be a special rule of life for all his brothers and sisters. Since the time of Francis, the greeting of Franciscans has been "Pax et Bonum!" "Peace and all good things to you!" "Peace and Goodness!" The memory of Francis can add a rich warmth to this greeting among Franciscans and as Franciscans greet others.

What Is Peace?

Peace is not simply pleasantness or the absence of problems, temptation or suffering. Christ had peace on the cross, and Mary had peace when she lost her son. The Church has peace even though it must always suffer. Saint Augustine's definition of peace is classic. He called peace the "tranquility of order." What he meant was that in order to have real peace, everything must be in its proper order. If our lives are governed by the laws of God's love, our relationship with God as well as with others is peaceful. And no matter what the disturbances on the surface of our life, as Christians, we can be peaceful with an inner serenity that nothing can take from us. Truly virtuous living is the key to peace. It should be obvious that such peace-having must precede any real peace-making.

The Virtues of Peacemaking

The peacemaker must be *humble*. When people are at each others' throats, they are in no mood to be lectured but they may be melted by the quiet presence of one from whom they have nothing to fear.

The peacemaker must be *charitable*. He is not trying to impose his will on anybody or to gain the reputation of being a clever arbiter. He is protecting truth and goodness. He is trying to create a little breathing space for God's love. The peacemaker must be prudent and patient. Saint Paul says: "If possible, have peace with every man." One must be ready to be silent when words are futile, forgiving when sarcasm would be the most satisfying, and patient when there is every reason to give up.

Sometimes we must be satisfied with a long-range program. Even if the couple next door are screaming at each other, they will close ranks against any outsider lecturing them. But a steady bombardment of gentleness, cheerfulness and kindness will soften their tensions and anger.

Peacemakers Must Be Christlike

All this is merely to say that Secular Franciscans must be Christlike in their peacemaking. "My peace I give unto you yet not as the world gives." The kind of peace Christ gives may sometimes be bought only at the price of pain. He said: "I have come not to bring peace but the sword." This means that the result of Christ's teaching will at times bring us face to face with malicious opposition. Then there will be an absence of that deceptive pleasantness on the surface, as there was on Calvary. But the peace of goodwill, which only God can give, will always be the mark of his children. Francis did not have peace with his own father but he had the peace of Christ.

As in war, peace is sometimes made by surrender—not by giving in on a principle but by yielding to the preferences of others. At times we may be forced to give in to keep peace. We must yield without bitterness or rancor, as Christ gave in to human power, with love and dignity.

The story of Francis and his followers is richly interwoven with instances of peacemaking. The Anthonys, Bernadines, Capistrans and Elizabeths of the Order are shining examples of the overflow of internal peace into the lives of others.

Questions for Reflection—What is peace? Why should a Franciscan make a special effort at peacemaking? What is the secret of peacemaking? What does "I have not come to bring peace but the sword" mean?

Connecting With Scripture and Franciscan Writings—Joshua, successor of Moses, in Joshua, Chapters 1, 2, 3, 6, 24. Bodo, pp. 116-118. Normile, *Following Francis of Assisi*, Chapter 6.

Application to Daily Life—What are your obligations to peacemaking?

149

Can you have peace in temptation? In suffering? In dryness of spirit? Is it cowardly to give in to keep peace? When? Is a long-range diplomacy of gentleness contrary to Franciscan simplicity? Remember: Peace depends on truth. Stick with the facts in keeping peace. Help make peace in the neighborhood by letting rumors and gossip die when they reach you. For your own peace, try to be always in union with God.

Prayer—Lord, make *me* an instrument of your peace....

From the Rule of the Secular Franciscan Order

19. Mindful that they are bearers of peace which must be built up unceasingly, they should seek out ways of unity and fraternal harmony through dialogue, trusting in the presence of the divine seed in everyone and in the transforming power of love and pardon.

    Messengers of perfect joy in every circumstance, they should strive to bring joy and hope to others.

    Since they are immersed in the resurrection of Christ, which gives true meaning to Sister Death, let them serenely tend toward the ultimate encounter with the Father.

REFLECTION 41

Caring for Creation

"God looked at everything he had made, and he found it very good."
—Genesis 1:31

Treasuring Creation

Saint Francis of Assisi was named the patron saint of ecology in 1989 for good reason. We might say that Francis saw with the eyes of God. He saw that all of creation was good, very good. Francis treasured each part of the created world that he viewed—from lofty Mt. Subasio where Assisi nestles to the tiniest worm creeping along the dusty road near his hometown. Francis believed that all creation was God's gift and was therefore to be treated as a treasure. In "The Canticle of the Creatures" Francis praises God for all creation—the sun and moon, the stars and the heavens, the wind and air, water and fire, flowers and fruits and herbs. Francis's heart overflowed with gratitude for all God's gifts.

Francis was following Jesus who also treasured creation to such extent that he used creation images as the basis for explaining spiritual truths to those who flocked to him. He spoke of seeds and sheep, figs and fields, pearls and plants, wheat and water. He spoke of these elements of creation to bring people closer to God.

Think for a moment of your most treasured possession. How do you care for it? Perhaps you look at it lovingly and handle it with care. You thank the one who gave it to you. You consider its meaning in your life. You use it with reverence. You choose not to use it in ways that might destroy it. Such is the way we are called to reverence all of creation that God has entrusted to us for our use.

The Irish poet Oscar Wilde wrote, "Where there is sorrow there is holy ground." When we view polluted waterways, forests devastated by acid rain or over-logging, abandoned junk piles, air thick with industrial and automotive wastes, and experience a sense of sorrow, that may be the beginning of recreating such areas as "holy ground." From our observation of the present condition of the earth comes the beginnings of change in how we choose to use God's precious gift of creation.

151

Ecology and Consumerism

Much emphasis is placed in our culture today on possessions. This emphasis is contrary to what Jesus taught. Jesus was so far removed from valuing possessions that he told his followers, "Foxes have holes, and birds of the air have nests, but the Son of Man has nowhere to lay his head" (Matthew 8:20). He did not even value a place to sleep at night. That's rather extreme, but then Christianity is extreme when weighed against the values of many cultures. Christianity moves us from self to others, from "me" to God. That move is reflected in our buying habits. No matter how little or how much material wealth we have at our disposal, we are called to use God's wisdom in determining how we spend it. We are not to judge others' ways but to thoughtfully, prayerfully consider how our habits affect the health of the earth.

A study concluded that a child born in the United States will consume one hundred times as much of the world's natural resources as a child born in a developing country. That's probably a very conservative estimate. Needless to say, we do not want children to exist as the poverty-stricken children of the developing world are often forced to do. Neither do we want to be the cause of the world's poverty by the manner in which we use its resources. No single, "right" answer exists. We must each search for our own answer through prayer, through learning about the fragile condition of the earth's environment, through observing our surroundings and our own habits. Then we must act in accord with the direction God gives us.

The Rule of the Secular Franciscan Order calls Franciscans to "universal kinship" with creation. That says we are all related to the universe and to each other. What is inflicted on the earth also wounds me and my family in some way through the chain of life that links us all. What is healed anywhere on the earth also promotes healing close to home.

Questions for Reflection—To whom does the earth belong? What have you done recently to improve the corner of the earth where you live? What is "enough" for you in terms of money? Possessions? Housing? How do you understand "universal kinship" as important to your life?

Connecting With Scripture and Franciscan Writings—Creation in Psalm 8; Bodo, *The Way of St. Francis*, pp. 123-132; Normile, Chapter 7.

Application to Daily Life—Find out where your community's trash and garbage are discarded and visit the site. How can you reduce how much you contribute to this accumulation by reducing what you purchase, by reusing when possible and by recycling whatever materials you can. Become an active advocate of reducing, reusing and recycling. Walk in a park or a peaceful, natural setting while reminding yourself: This is holy ground. Share your thoughts about this walk with a friend.

What one thing can you begin to do differently today to preserve or restore a bit of creation?

Prayer—All praise be yours, my Lord,
        through Sister Earth, our mother,
        who feeds us in her sovereignty
        and produces various fruits with coloured flowers and herbs.
        Amen. (Saint Francis, "The Canticle of the Creatures")

From the Rule of the Secular Franciscan Order

18. Moreover they should respect all creatures, animate and inanimate, which "bear the imprint of the Most High," and they should strive to move from the temptation of exploiting creation to the Franciscan concept of universal kinship.

REFLECTION 42

Work: A Joint Venture in Creation

*"You shall eat the fruit of the labor of your hands;
you shall be happy, and it shall go well with you"*

—Psalm 128:2

"Anyone unwilling to work should not eat."

—1 Thessalonians 3:10

*"Everyone should remain in the trade and
in the position in which he was called....
Always be doing something worthwhile;
then the devil will always find you busy."*

—Saint Jerome, Epistle 125

Work Is a Gift

If we're exhausted from a long day's difficult labor, we may question the notion that work is a gift. It may not always seem like a gift. However, consider the alternatives when one does not have the opportunity to work: unemployment, hopelessness, homelessness, inability to care for self and family. Those who face such conditions know how frightening it is not to be able to work. One of the frustrations of illness or injury is the inability to work in our usual manner.

When we work, we use the gifts God has given us. Perhaps a strong body is the gift that enables you to do manual labor. An inquisitive mind may lead you to become a scientist, teacher or writer. A great sensitivity to people's needs may place you in social work or enable you to parent more effectively. Whatever work we do, as long as it does not cause scandal and does not lead us from being faithful followers of Jesus, is God's gift to us.

Gifts are not given to us for ourselves alone. I don't work to have more and more for *me!* Work is a gift we receive. Work is a gift we give. We use our gifts to continue God's work of creation and in doing so

God continues to create us. To discover our talents and abilities and to use them productively helps us to discover ourselves. As tiny infants we discovered our fingers. Then we discovered what those little fingers could do. They could pick up a piece of banana or hold onto Dad's finger. Later those same fingers may have learned to play the flute or hold a baseball bat. Perhaps during their lives those fingers operate a computer or design buildings or perform surgery. *Play* is a child's *work* through which he discovers his own special giftedness which continues to create the world.

As we begin each day, we can express thanks to God for the work before us, for the gift of talent that enables us to perform our work, for the people we will work with, for the results of our labor which we cannot yet see. If our work is not gratifying to us, we might ask God for the ability to develop our gifts in new directions. We must then be willing to work toward our own development through training and education.

Francis and Work

When Francis heard God's call, it was "to go and rebuild my Church." Because Francis was not afraid of physical work, he immediately began to restore small churches in the Umbrian plain. He gathered and hauled stones, begged for other materials and used the strength of his muscle and the sweat of his brow to patch crumbling walls and replace collapsing roofs. He worked.

Later in his life, one might think that Francis had an aversion to work because he insisted that his little brothers beg for food and seek shelter in abandoned places rather than building houses for themselves, rather than earning a wage with which to go to the market or rent a place to live. However, the friars were encouraged to continue at whatever vocation they had pursued before becoming followers of Francis. For wages they were permitted to accept anything essential for their daily needs *except* money. Work was gift to those for whom the labor was done. Wages in the form of food or clothing were gifts from those who benefited from the labor of Francis' followers. They were cautioned not to allow their work to interfere with their spiritual lives. They "should work in a spirit of faith and devotion and avoid idleness, which is the enemy of the soul, without however extinguishing the spirit of prayer and devotion, to which every temporal consideration must be subordinate" (Saint Francis, *Omnibus*, p. 61).

As married couples, those with families chose to follow the way of Francis, the restriction on receiving wages in the form of money was altered. While the responsibilities of the laity were equal in terms of never allowing work to diminish the spirit of prayer and devotion, wages in the form of money were permitted.

The place where we work—in an office, on a construction site, in our home, in a store or hospital—these are the places we are called to live 'Gospel to life, life to the Gospel.' We *live* the gospel where we work and where we work challenges us to learn the gospel way more fully. The wages received in return for work performed can be used in creative ways for the betterment of others who may be less fortunate than we are. Secular Franciscans today understand that earning a living is an honorable way of life, a way of using one's God-given gifts. To work is to become co-creator with God.

Making Work Our Play

Francis made his work his play. Walking along the roads of Umbria, Francis spread his charism of joy. He sang—often in French, the language of the troubadours he admired—as he went to tend the lepers in their isolated hideaways. He played his imaginary fiddle made of sticks as he went from town to town preaching the gospel he so loved. He was doing God's work! Perhaps if we think of our work as our way of doing God's work, if we think of our work as our play, we will find more joy in serving as workers. We might sing songs of praise on our daily commute to work. We may pray silent prayers of joyful thanksgiving throughout the day. We might look for opportunities to smile at others and to laugh with coworkers or customers. We can become Francis in our own marketplaces.

Questions for Reflection—How does your attitude at work reflect your Christian way of life? What excuses do you make for not living in a Christian way? How do joyful workers empower you to work in a more productive, joyful way?

Connecting With Scripture and Franciscan Writings—Timothy, Chapters 1 and 11; Bodo, *The Way of St. Francis* pp. 9-14; Normile, pp. 37-43.

Application to Daily Life—For a week, keep a record of what brings you joy in your work and what robs you of joy. Give thanks for the former; ask God's help with the latter. Each day ask yourself how your work has contributed to God's ongoing creation of the world. As you read newspapers or watch television, reflect on how work is used to set people free or to imprison them. What can you do to make a difference where individuals are "prisoners" to their work?

Prayer—Dear God, when I'm tired from a day's work, help me to remember that work is your gift. I am graced with the privilege of toil which continues your work of creation. Thank you for the skills and talents you have given for my work. Amen.

From the Rule of the Secular Franciscan Order

16. Let them esteem work both as a gift and as a sharing in the creation, redemption and service of the human community.

REFLECTION 43

Charity for the Sick

"The 'Canticle of [the Creatures],' for all the depth it displays towards creatures, is nonetheless an earnest prayer. What makes it all the more remarkable is the fact that, written though it was during his last illness and amid intense suffering, it displays a heart filled with joy and happiness and a heart filled with the deepest gratitude toward almighty God, even for suffering and for Sister Death."

—Omnibus

Companions of the Suffering Christ

Before considering how we should treat the sick, we should consider the Christian meaning of suffering itself. In themselves, sickness and suffering are tragic and senseless, the inheritance of original sin. But Christ has sanctified even the wounds of human nature. This terrible scourge of mankind can be changed into a blessing, by being united to the sufferings of Christ.

The Mystical Body Continues the Life of the Suffering Christ

Many people feel that this sublime privilege does not count for them. They are not good enough. Their sickness is not that important. They believe it is a punishment. But Christ does want to take your individual suffering, headache, arthritis or cancer and unite it to his. Remember, "the head cannot say to the hand, 'I have no need of you.'" Of all the statements about our continuing Christ's life, none is more astounding that this: "I fill up in my body for what is wanting in the suffering of Christ, for the sake of his body, which is the Church." Our Father Francis received the highest proof of Christ's love and need of him when his body was literally put on a cross with Christ by the reality of the five wounds of the stigmata.

Why Did Christ Suffer?

The Son of God entered into the human misery that had resulted from sin. He let evil seem to overcome him, going down even into death like anyone else. But the human Christ who did this was totally possessed by the love of his Father and this love was infinitely more powerful than all the forces of evil. Christ maintained his perfect trust no matter what happened to him. He was totally in the hands of his Father.

All the suffering brothers and sisters of Christ are asked to become part of Christ's great act of love on the cross by continuing it and offering it as a substitute for all the sins ever committed. "Beloved, do not be surprised at the fiery ordeal that is taking place among you to test you, as though something strange were happening to you. But rejoice insofar as you are sharing Christ's sufferings, so that you may also be glad and shout for joy when his glory is revealed" (1 Peter 4:12-13).

The Joy of Francis

Franciscan tradition calls us to maintain the spirit of Francis especially in suffering. Secular Franciscans who are sick, disabled or afflicted with any infirmity are not to see these afflictions as punishments of God but as results of living in physical human bodies. We are to seek healing offered through the skills of the medical profession which are also God's gifts. We are to call on the prayers of the community for healing. We can request the Anointing of the Sick. And in the manner of Francis, we will remember these words in order to maintain our sense of joy even in suffering: "I beg the sick brother to thank God for everything and to desire to be whatever the Lord wills, whether sick or well" (Saint Francis, *Earlier Rule*).*

The Sick Are Valuable Members of the Mystical Body

Perhaps the greatest thing a man or woman does in life is to co-suffer with Christ in sickness. The sick make giant strides in holiness and the Mystical Body is benefited. They must never think that they are useless. Christ achieved his greatest work when he was hopeless and "useless" on the Cross.

Vatican II has some particularly impressive words about the sick: "By the sacred anointing of the sick and the prayer of her priests the whole Church commends those who are ill to the suffering and glorified Lord, asking that he may lighten their suffering and save them. She exhorts them, moreover, to contribute to the welfare of the whole

---

* When the original author of this book, Father Leonard Foley, O.F.M., was diagnosed with cancer and given a short time to live, he told his friends, "Never forget—God is good and life is wonderful!" His cancer may have been terminal but his joy was eternal!

People of God by associating themselves freely with the passion and death of Christ" ("The Church," No. 11).

It should be noted that the Sacrament of Anointing of the Sick is for those who are sick with no necessary implication that they are dying. All Catholics should make an effort to adopt this healthy attitude toward the sacrament and help blot out once and for all the false idea that receiving the sacrament is a sort of death warrant.

Francis and the Sick

Saint Francis showed his tender regard for the sick by making an exception in one of his strictest rules:

> Let none of the brothers, therefore, wherever he may be or go, carry, receive, or have received in any way coin or money, whether for clothing, books, or payment for some work—indeed, not for any reason, unless for an evident need of the sick brothers.... They must rejoice when they live among people considered of little value and looked down upon, among the poor and the powerless, the sick and the lepers...

> If any of the brothers falls sick, wherever he may be, let the other brothers not leave him behind unless one of the brothers, or even several of them, if necessary, is designated to serve him as "they would want to be served themselves." ...I beg the sick brother to thank God for everything. (Saint Francis, Earlier Rule)

The tradition of the Secular Franciscan Order of Saint Francis places great stress on charity toward the sick and infirm. Francis saw the Christ of the Gospels not only preaching the Kingdom to people's minds and hearts but also going out of his way to relieve the pain and sickness of their bodies. And Francis could do no less! To be very practical, then, Secular Franciscans must make it a matter of special concern to visit the sick and infirm, with sympathy, encouragement and fraternal charity. Nothing could be closer to the mind of Saint Francis than to see Christ in the sick and to relieve his pain. The merit of suffering is only increased by the smiles we can bring to the faces of the sick and through the encouragement our sympathy brings to their hearts. Most of all, our prayers bring them strength to continue their present task in the Mystical Body.

Questions for Reflection—What can Christians do for those who are sick? What actually is offered to God in times of suffering?

Connecting With Scripture and Franciscan Writings—God and his covenant in Deuteronomy, Chapter 4:44-49, Chapters 5-11. Bodo, pp. 118-119.

Application to Daily Life—Whether healthy or sick, try to see suffering and sickness in its union with the suffering and victorious Christ. Try to visit or contact through a note or phone call at least one sick or homebound person this week. Bring a small gift. Offer your services for a task the individual may need done.

Prayer—Lord, your life on earth was filled with concern for the sick. Have compassion now on all who share your pain. Give them healing of mind and body; restore their strength and spirit. May they be comforted by the knowledge that we are praying for them and find peace in a sense of your presence. May they know that in a special way they are united with your suffering. May they contribute to the welfare of the whole people of God by associating themselves freely with your passion and death for the salvation of the world. Bless those who take care of the sick. In their own time of need, may they receive a hundredfold the blessings they have given (Leonard Foley, O.F.M., in Patti Normile, *Prayers for Caregivers*, p. 78).

The Apostolate: 'Repair My Church'

"When he heard that Christ's disciples should not possess gold or silver or money, or carry on their journey a wallet or a sack, nor bread...but that they should preach the kingdom of God and penance, the holy man, Francis, immediately exulted in the spirit of God. 'This is what I want,' he said, 'this is what I seek, this is what I desire with all my heart.'"

—Celano, The Life of Saint Francis

The index of the paperback edition of Vatican II documents has 153 references to "apostolate." Even allowing for some duplication, we are certainly being forcibly reminded that to be Christian is to be apostolic. To receive the riches of Christ is to want to share them.

Because Christian life and the apostolate cannot be separated, we may say that this whole book is about the apostolate. But let us take a last overall view of the apostolate within the Church and of our call to unify and expand all Christianity.

"Repair My Church"

One of the great turning points of Francis's life was the occasion when Christ spoke to him from the crucifix. He had been walking near the little church of San Damiano. He was sad at its crumbling, unkempt condition and went in to pray before the altar. As he prayed, he heard a voice speaking to him from the crucifix: "Francis, go and repair my Church which as you see is wholly in ruin."

He was startled. His Master had spoken to him! He took the words to mean the poor little church on that spot and in his humility he quickly replied, "Gladly, Lord, will I repair it." If the rest of his life had been spent doing nothing but repairing the stones of that or any dilapidated church, he would have been supremely happy. It was nothing, but it was for the Lord. It was only later that it became evident that it was the

Church of Christ that Francis was to repair, not physical structures but the spiritual foundation.

The Dream of Pope Innocent III

Great benefits to the Church would come from this ragged band of gospel minstrels who gathered around Francis. But the Holy Father was at first repulsed when Francis came to him. It was almost against his will that he finally was attracted to the poor little man from Assisi. He remembered a dream which he had. The Mother Church of Christendom, Saint John Lateran, was tottering on its foundations. A religious person, small of stature and unimpressive in appearance, came and held it up by setting his back against it. The Pope realized that Francis was this man and gave the first approval to the new Order.

Reform by Those Who Need It

The Church is ourselves, Christ united with his members. We are the glory and the shame of the Church. The constant purification of the Church, therefore, must be done by those who make up the Church and who need purification, that is, by you and me. We spoil what God has made. Therefore, the purifying, too, must begin in ourselves. Even our penance is not a private affair. We are all in this together, allowing God to purify and reform us and others and the Church.

The Apostolate Within the Parish

The Secular Franciscan must always be conscious of the world-wide Mystical Body of Christ. But Secular Franciscans will find their most practical and beneficial apostolate within their own parish. This means cooperating, first of all, in its activities. If Secular Franciscans are to promote practices of spiritual devotion and good works, they should be most faithful in attending the liturgies of the Church: attending Mass daily, if possible; receiving the sacraments frequently; being present for special services and devotional times; parish renewals; weddings and funerals.

But perhaps the greatest reform needed in the Church today is the acceptance of the idea of reform. Vatican II began in a blaze of glory, but its promise and ideals have not substantially changed the attitude of many Catholics. Decades later, polarization between liberals and conservatives, new and old emphases in theology, and similar issues continue to be scandals in the Church. If there was ever a peacemaking task for Secular Franciscans, it is in building up their parishes, striving for harmony where differences threaten to divide the Church.

Teaching About the Catholic Faith

Churches are in need of laity to teach catechism to children attending public schools. The parish requires the services of qualified teachers for its own school. The Confraternity of Christian Doctrine is an example of an essential apostolate of the Church, localized within each parish, in which many Secular Franciscans can find an outlet for their zeal. The need for continuing adult religious education is ongoing. Training is offered through diocesan education offices and through Lay Pastoral Ministry Programs offered throughout the country.

Helping Converts

Parishes need lay people to guide those non-Catholics who are exploring the Catholic faith through the Rite of Christian Initiation of Adults (RCIA). Lay persons can be of great help in sharing what their faith means to them. They may answer questions which non-Catholics might not ask a priest. All Catholics should show a special friendliness to converts who may feel strange and alone in a new church. They may find it difficult to come to church alone. They may feel self-conscious about many things in the rituals of the Church. Simple friendliness can do untold good.

Helping Sinners

"We are sent," says Saint Francis, "to heal the wounds, to tend the maimed, and to bring back those who have lost their way." As long as there is one sinner on earth, Francis would be restless.

So Franciscans should show a special kindness to those who have strayed from the protecting mantle of the Church—whether because of misunderstanding, anger, invalid marriage or any other reason. The farther they are from the Church, the more they need the kindness of Christ. The friendly greeting of one Catholic man or woman may be the only link with the faith of their childhood. God can use this as a grace to bring them back. It may take many years, but charity never fails.

Christ Is the Soul of the Apostolate

On one occasion when Francis became discouraged, Christ said to him, "Tell me, you simple and ignorant little man, why do you grieve so when a brother leaves the Order and the brothers do not follow the way I showed you? Tell me, then, who has founded this community? Who converts them to penitence?" It is Christ alone who is the missionary. He works through us, and he succeeds only to the degree that he can create his life in us first.

Questions for Reflection—What actually is the "Good News"? How is it proclaimed within the Church?

Connecting With Scripture and Franciscan Writings—Joshua, successor of Moses, in Joshua, Chapters 1, 2, 3, 6, 24. Normile, *Following Francis of Assisi*, Chapter 3.

Application to Daily Life—What is the greatest need in your parish? Are you "old Church" or "new Church?" Are you willing to listen to others' views of the Church? Read your parish bulletin and seriously consider offering your services in an area where you can help strengthen your community of the faithful.

Prayer—I'm listening, Lord Jesus. What part of your Church would you have me rebuild? Show me the way. Amen.

The Apostolate:
That All May Be One

"I beseech all my brothers whether clergy or lay, whether engaged in preaching or in prayer or in labor, to aim at keeping humble in everything; not to boast, nor be pleased with themselves nor interiorly elated, at the good words or deeds, or anything good which God says or does or accomplishes in them or through them."

—*Saint Francis*

Ecumenism

One of the surprising results of the window-opening by Pope John XXIII has been the ecumenical movement. Instead of thinking of Protestants as "the enemy," most Catholics now see an already-existing unity of Christians. While it does not reflect perfect unity, it is to be treasured and reinforced. This is a much better focus than emphasizing our differences. A long and challenging path lies ahead, but we have progressed. At least we are beginning to remove the scandal that seventy percent of the world—the number who do not believe in Christ—saw in a divided Christianity.

Pope John Paul II, when asked about the plurality of religions in the world refocused the question and replied, "Instead I will attempt to show the *common fundamental element* and the *common root* of these religions" (*Crossing the Threshold of Hope*, p. 44). We are called to do the same—seek what we have in common with those of other faiths. At the same time we must faithfully and lovingly live our Christian/Catholic/Franciscan faith.

The Statements of Vatican II

If possible, everyone should study at least an outline of the *Decree on Ecumenism* of Vatican II. Here we can quote only a few excerpts:

Every renewal of the Church consists essentially in an increase of fidelity to her own calling.... Christ summons his Church to that con-

166

tinual reformation of which she is always in need, insofar as she is an institution of men here on earth.

...There can be no ecumenism worthy of the name without a change of heart. For it is from newness of attitudes, from self-denial and unstinted love, that yearnings for unity take their rise and grow toward maturity. We should therefore pray to the Holy Spirit for the grace to be genuinely self-denying, humble, gentle in the service of others, and to have an attitude of brotherly generosity toward them.

...Let all Christ's faithful remember that the more purely they strive to live according to the Gospel, the more they are fostering and even practicing Christian unity. For they can achieve depth and ease in strengthening mutual brotherhood to the degree that they enjoy profound communion with the Father, the Word, and the Spirit ("Decree on Ecumenism," No. 5-7).

What Is Necessary to Spread the Faith?

Secular Franciscans should be informed Catholics. Many Catholics feel that they do not know enough to talk about religion. However, they may know more than they realize and may merely be timid. Others may think they know a great deal about their Church when, in fact, they have not learned about the faith since their school days. They should give themselves a trial. If they are knowledgeable, they can build on that knowledge. If they really are ignorant of their faith, they have an obligation to learn more, for their own sake. In either case, those who appreciate their faith will want to share it with others. People never tire of enthusiastically inviting others to a cause they deeply believe in.

Modern Needs

Furthermore, we should be as much up-to-date as possible on the modern needs that call for gospel principles for their solution. Reading the diocesan newspaper and one or two Catholic magazines is informative. We should be aware of discussions and movements within the Church, the statements of the Holy Father and of the bishops. We should be conscious of the problems of the society in which we live. Principles do not change, but there are shifting sets of circumstances to which principles are to be applied. Cloning, *in vitro* fertilization, the ethics of organ transplants are a few of the issues that challenge Catholic morality today.

Say What Is True and Good

Christianity is spread by the Holy Spirit. Saint Paul said, "My speech and my proclamation were not with plausible words of wisdom, but with a demonstration of the Spirit and of power" (1 Corinthians 2:4).

We do the faith more harm than good if we seem intent only on crushing opponents in arguments. Besides, arguments are useless when emotion is aroused.

We can do many things to spread the faith. Listen respectfully to others who ask about our faith. Explain beliefs and practices of the faith to those who ask, why did you go to Mass this morning, a weekday? What is the Mass, anyway? What is that smudge on your forehead? What is penance? What do you do when you receive the Sacrament of Reconciliation?

Out of the fullness of the heart the mouth speaks. If you are full of the faith, you will unconsciously and automatically apply it lovingly to all situations. And you will thus be preaching the gospel, without being "preachy." Think of the long-range effect if your comments on daily events run something like this: "I hope he gets another chance." "No, I don't care for another drink." "Let's stop and say hello." "Maybe they didn't know any better." "I will be glad to do it for you." "I am going to vote for him because he is honest and competent." "Isn't it a wonderful day?" "You certainly have done a good job." "Let's wait until we've all cooled down to settle this."

Questions for Reflection—What is a herald? What are the obvious requirements of one who announces good news? What is the name of your diocesan newspaper? What features do you like best in it? What should be our attitude towards our separated brethren? How can you spread the faith in ordinary conversation? Are you as well informed about your faith as about your job, fashions, cars, sports, entertainers, the stock market? Would an evangelical Christian be envious of your zeal?

Connecting With Scripture and Franciscan Writings—Samuel the prophet in 1 Kings, Chapters 1-8. Bodo, *The Way of St. Francis*, pp. 63-68.

Application to Daily Life—Search for the proof that your belief in Christianity shows in your daily life. Can people where you work depend on you for straight information about the faith? Practice with a friend or family member how to explain to non-Catholics: a) the essentials of the Sacrament of Reconciliation; b) why the Mass is the center of Christianity. If some public figure makes a false statement about the faith in your town, write a note kindly stating the truth the Church holds.

Prayer—Someone I know needs you in their life, Lord. Give me the faith and courage to speak up for you and invite them into your love. Amen.

REFLECTION *46*

The Apostolate of Good Example

"All Brothers ought to preach by their actions."
—Saint Francis

The Christian life, the apostolate, living the gospel can be described in many ways. The one which best fits every man's values and judgment is "good example."

Whether we are speaking of virtue or sin, it is true that attitude is all-important. We are what we decide to be, by an ongoing and basic decision. But it is also true that our deepest attitudes must express themselves and they do. One does not keep up "good example" very long unless it is the fruit of a genuine inner commitment.

A Powerful Influence

We sometimes think that we have little influence on others. They seem to pay little or no attention to us. Yet, let us look at our own lives. After the grace of God, all the goodness we have is the result of good example. We have been powerfully influenced for good by our mothers and fathers, teachers and friends and the ever-widening circle of good people whom we meet in life. We are influenced by the example of those who have gone before us. We remember particular instances: being greatly encouraged to pray by seeing a friend making the Way of the Cross, marveling at the silent endurance of injury by a friend, seeing silent and Christlike suffering, seeing courageous defense of someone being persecuted.

Faithfulness of Example

The example of others influences us most. We may be moved for the moment by some unusual and spectacular action of another. But the influences that affect us most deeply are those which continue day after day, year after year. Constant good example formed our character. The sight of Dad going to Communion every Sunday is a picture that will never be forgotten and will never cease to encourage us to do the same. The memory of Mom taking a basket of dinner to a sick neighbor will inspire us to do the same.

What You Are

Someone once said: "What you are thunders so loud, I can't hear what you say! " We can only influence others by what we are. We may playact for a while, but sooner or later everyone knows exactly what and who we are. We must examine our external conduct but this will bring us face to face with our interior spirit. If we take care of the inner peace that comes from living close to Christ, we will have no trouble giving good example. When others see us, they will see Christ.

The Example of Francis

A story in one of the earliest biographies of Francis describes the power of his example and the great spirit that attracted everyone to him. At one of the meetings of the friars, it was said that "if one of the brothers was undergoing an inner struggle or fighting against a temptation, it sufficed for him to see Saint Francis, to hear him speak with loving zeal, to witness the sacrifices he made—and all temptations and all sadness miraculously vanished, for he spoke to them with great compassion, not as a judge, but as a loving father to his sons, or a good physician to his patients" *(Legend of the Three Companions)*.

Where Is Good Example Needed?

Pope John Paul II reminded the faithful "of the universal call to holiness in the Church. This vocation is universal and concerns each of the baptized, every Christian. It is always very personal, connected to work, to one's profession. It is an account rendered of the talents each person has received—whether one has made good or bad use of them. We know that the words the Lord Jesus spoke about the man who had buried the talent were very harsh and threatening [cf. Matthew 25:25-30]" *(Crossing the Threshold of Hope*, p. 180).

Years before, Pope Pius XII said: "I cannot go into [all] the factories, the shops, the offices and mines. Thousands of...lay missionaries are needed to represent the Church in their working environment." We must fight the sinfulness of the world, but not by withdrawing from the conflict. We join, we become involved in, the activities of the world that we may put the spirit of Christ into them. In theaters and newspaper offices, in washrooms and supermarkets, in colleges and hospitals and restaurants, we must be Christ to everyone. We must be, in these circumstances, what Christ would be in them. We must do what he would do.

Questions for Reflection—Who has influenced you the most in the way you live your life? What is it in others that encourages you to live your Christian life more faithfully? Whom are you influencing? How?

Connecting With Scripture and Franciscan Writings—Saul, the first king in 1 Kings, Chapters 9-16. Bodo, *The Way of St. Francis*, pp. 105-106.

Application to Daily Life—Perhaps our influence on others—children, friends, fellow workers, neighbors—is greater than we realize. Think of some action you have performed recently and consider how your act influenced others positively...or negatively. Remember that if you allow God to possess your mind and heart, good example will take care of itself. Act on the knowledge that you influence people most by unfailing faithfulness to daily duties in the spirit of Christ.

Prayer—Please, Lord, keep me from being a hypocrite. I want to live my belief in you with honesty. Show me the secret corners of my life that I try to hide from others and from you. Amen.

REFLECTION 47

Perfect Joy

"May I never boast of anything except the cross of Our Lord Jesus Christ..."
—Galatians 6:14

A classic story comes from that delightful book of Franciscan tradition called the *Fioretti—The Little Flowers of Saint Francis*—which every Secular Franciscan should know, because it summarizes the spirit of Francis.

Not Holiness

One winter day, Saint Francis was returning to Saint Mary of the Angels from Perugia with Brother Leo. The bitter cold made them suffer keenly. Saint Francis called to Brother Leo, who was walking a bit ahead of him and said: "Brother Leo, even if the Friars Minor in every country give a great example of holiness and integrity and good edification, nevertheless write down and note carefully that perfect joy is not in that."

Not Miracles

And when he had walked on a bit, Saint Francis called again saying: "Brother Leo, even if a Friar Minor gives sight to the blind, heals the paralyzed, drives out devils, gives hearing back to the deaf, makes the lame walk, and restores speech to the dumb, and what is still more, brings back to life a man who has been dead four days, write that perfect joy is not in that."

Not Knowledge

And going on a bit, Francis cried out again in a strong voice: "Brother Leo, if a Friar Minor knows all languages and all sciences and Scripture, if he also knows how to prophesy and to reveal not only the future but also the secrets of the consciences and minds of others, write down and note carefully that perfect joy is not in that."

And as they walked on, after a while Francis called again forcefully: "Brother Leo, Little Lamb of God, even if a Friar Minor could speak with the voice of an angel and knew the courses of the stars and the powers of herbs and knew all about the treasures in the earth, and if he knew the qualities of birds and fishes, animals, humans, roots, trees, rocks and waters, write down and note carefully that true joy is not in that."

Not Preaching

And going on a bit farther, Saint Francis called again strongly: "Brother Leo, even if a Friar Minor could preach so well that he should convert all infidels to the faith of Christ, write that perfect joy is not there."

Perfect Joy...

Now when he had been talking this way for a distance of two miles, Brother Leo in great amazement asked him: "Father, I beg you in God's name to tell me where perfect joy is."

And Saint Francis replied: "When we come to Saint Mary of the Angels, soaked by the rain and frozen by the cold, all soiled with mud and suffering from hunger, and we ring at the gate of the place and the brother porter comes and says angrily: 'Who are you?' And we say: 'We are two of your brothers.' And he contradicts us, saying: 'You are not telling the truth. Rather you are two rascals who go around deceiving people and stealing what they give to the poor. Go away!' And he does not open for us, but makes us stand outside in the snow and rain, cold and hungry, until night falls—then if we endure all those insults and cruel rebuffs patiently, without being troubled and without complaining, and if we reflect humbly and charitably that the porter really knows us and that God makes him speak against us, oh, Brother Leo, write that perfect joy is there!"

And Again...

"And if we continue to knock, and the porter comes out in anger and drives us away with curses and hard blows like bothersome scoundrels, saying: 'Get away from here, you dirty thieves—go to the hospital! Who do you think you are? You certainly won't eat or sleep here!' and if we bear it patiently and take the insults with joy and love in our heart, Brother Leo, write that perfect joy is there!"

And Again

"And if later, suffering intensely from hunger and painful cold, with night falling, we still knock and call, and crying loudly beg them to open for us and let us come in for the love of God, and he grows still more angry and says: 'Those fellows are bold and shameless ruffians. I'll give them what they deserve!'

And he comes out with a knotty club, and grasping us by the cowl throws us onto the ground, rolling us in the mud and snow and beats us with the club so much that he covers our bodies with wounds—if we endure all those evils and insults and blows with joy and patience, reflecting that we must accept and bear the sufferings of the Blessed Christ patiently for love of him, oh, Brother Leo, write: that is perfect joy!"

"And now hear the conclusion, Brother Leo. Above all the graces and gifts of the Holy Spirit which Christ gives to his friends is that of conquering oneself and willingly enduring sufferings, insults, humiliations, and hardships for the love of Christ. For we cannot glory in all those other marvelous gifts of God, as they are not ours but God's as the Apostle says: 'What have you that you have not received?'

"But we can glory in the cross of tribulations and afflictions, because that is ours, and so the Apostle says: 'I will not glory save in the Cross of Our Lord Jesus Christ!'"

Questions for Reflection—What phrase sums up Saint Francis's description of perfect joy? What is the motive to seeing perfect joy as Francis saw it?

Connecting With Scripture and Franciscan Writings—David, the early days, in 1 Kings, Chapters 17-24. Normile, *Following Francis of Assisi*, Chapter 8.

Application to Daily Life—What is the greatest suffering you must endure today? What is your greatest personal cross? When a painful situation arises, try to remember the story of perfect joy and apply it as Christ inspires you to do.

Prayer—True joy guides my life toward you, dear God. Joy can come even in times of sadness because you are with me in the pain and suffering. You are my joy! Amen.

Structure

*T*he Franciscan family, as one among many spiritual families raised up by the Holy Spirit in the Church, unites all members of the People of God—laity, religious, and priests—who recognize that they are called to follow Christ in the footsteps of Saint Francis of Assisi.

In various ways and forms but in life-giving union with each other, they intend to make present the charism of their common Seraphic Father in the life and mission of the Church.

REFLECTION 48

Fraternity as Community

"[A]fter the Lord gave me some brothers, no one showed me what I had to do, but the Most High Himself revealed to me that I should live according to the pattern of the Holy Gospel."

—Saint Francis, The Testament

Francis as a young man treasured his relationships with his friends. They reveled together, partied together, even went to war together. When Francis discovered Lady Poverty and first heard the Lord's call to "go and rebuild my Church," he entered a period of life of aloneness. He left friends and family behind because he knew they could not understand his call. Indeed, at this time he did not understand it himself. Those who did not understand his need to search for meaning might hold him back, deter him from what was most important to him. During this period of his life he meandered through the Umbrian countryside as a solitary wanderer, searching for understanding of his call from Jesus and seeking to know himself. Alone, he entered the caves of Mount Subasio to pray, perhaps to call out to God where no one else could hear his shouts of pain and confusion when the dream seemed unclear.

But Francis could not remain alone for two reasons. He was a "people person" and the Lord is also a "people person." These reasons created Francis into a kind of human magnet to others who observed his way of life and who experienced his spiritual growth. He could not have remained alone if he had wanted to. The life he had chosen was simply too attractive to others who loved the Lord.

Bernard of Quintavalle was Francis's first follower. Bernard had what many people think of as essentials for happiness—wealth and respected social position in the town of Assisi. But Bernard lacked the joy in life that he witnessed in the "new" Francis.

So Bernard invited Francis to his home for supper and a night's rest, since Francis now had no home to call his own. As evening came, Francis feigned sleep, then spent the night in prayer. Witnessing, without Francis's knowing, the intensity and humility of his prayer, "My God and my all!" repeated through the night and dawn hours, Bernard knew Francis to be a genuine and faithful follower of the Lord. And with daybreak came the dawn of the Franciscan order: Francis had his first follower.

Neither man knew that a movement that would extend across centuries and around the world would result from their friendship with each other and with Jesus. They were now simply two rather than one in love with Lady Poverty setting out to rebuild the Church of Jesus Christ. Others clamored to be around them because they were good, they were joyful, they were men of God. The two became thousands. The unmarried men were joined by women, married men, by families. If this had not happened, the Franciscan charism might have lingered a few years after Francis's death in 1226. It might have been captured in history books. It might have become a blessed memory in Church history. But because two, then ten, then hundreds and thousands joined Francis, the Franciscan way exists today, not in books and memories but in the lives of men, women and children around the globe.

For that reason, those who are called to follow Francis are called to fraternity as community. The word *fraternity* does not exclude women. It means that Jesus is our brother. We are also called to be brothers and sisters to Jesus with Francis and his other followers. Fraternity keeps us from becoming self-centered. Fraternity creates the place where apostolic work in the world is fostered. Fraternity gives us strength where we are weak. Fraternity gives us opportunities to love others with all their goodness as well as their flaws and irritating ways. And they can do the same for us. Fraternity provides an intimate spiritual family within the larger spiritual family of Church where we can grow in holiness according to God's command, "You shall be holy, for I am holy" (1 Peter 1:16).

The Secular Franciscan Order formerly had "isolated" members. These members were Franciscans who followed the way of Francis on their own without the benefit of fraternity. In some cases geographic distances made this seem desirable. However, members now are linked with fraternities located geographically as near to them as possible. Where distance is a hindrance, members are encouraged to travel distances for times of fraternal gatherings or to invite others into fraternity with them. We go the Franciscan way together, not as individuals on private journeys.

In fraternity we are reminded of our Franciscan charism. Meeting regularly provides opportunities to work together. Individuals grow in friendship in the Lord and each other as they pray together, work together, motivate each other, share their faith journeys. Fraternities are havens of joy where laughter and humor lighten life's burdens. Fraternities provide a place to learn to resolve disagreements peaceably. Fraternities are places to learn to forgive ourselves and others as we begin again and again to follow Francis and Jesus.

Questions for Reflection—Why is fraternity necessary to live the authentic Franciscan way of life? What aspects of Franciscan fraternity life might be helpful to your faith journey? What might you do if the Franciscan fraternity you belong to or are considering joining seems lacking in enthusiasm? (Remember this word comes from *"en theos"* meaning "in God.")

Connecting With Scriptures and Franciscan Writings—Community life in Acts 2:46-47; Bodo, *Tales of St. Francis: Ancient Stories for Contemporary Living*, pp. 36-41, 120-122.

Application to Daily Life—If you are searching for a Franciscan fraternity whose members might help you on your faith journey, inquire of Franciscans in your area or call 1-800-FRANCIS for information. If you already belong to a Franciscan fraternity, arrange to discuss at one of your gatherings how your fraternity might improve its spirit of fraternal community.

Prayer—Lord, sometimes the temptation to strike out on my own is very strong. I can't see how my present life with my family, or my brothers and sisters in community, is allowing me to grow. Everyone around me seems only a distraction or a burden, and I wish I could just leave everything and everyone and be free. But that is only a temptation most of the time, Lord. For I find you in my commitments and responsibilities, my loves and friendships, not in fleeing them. And in finding you, I find myself. You are where I am, not somewhere else. Lord Jesus, help me to discover you where I am. Amen (*Tales of St. Francis*, p. 122).

Organization of the Secular Franciscan Order

"The Seraphic Father Francis wished his ministers to be courteous to their subjects, kindly and gentle.... He wished them to be reasonable in their commands, forgiving in the face of offenses, more ready to bear than to return injuries, to be enemies of sin but physicians of sinners. Finally he wished them to be such that their lives would be a mirror of disciplined living. On the other hand, he wished them to be treated with all honor and to be loved, seeing that they had to bear the burden of cares and labors" [cf. Matthew 20:12].

—*Celano*, The Life of Saint Francis

Saint Francis and Organization

Francis himself had little knack for organization. He was a free spirit, guided by the Spirit of God, drawing men to follow him by the sheer force of his gospel life. He thought of spirit rather than law, the burning urgency of inspired Christians rather than the more prosaic caution of experience. But he himself recognized that thousands of Franciscans could no longer live according to a few simple rules. Something was needed to keep some order in the Franciscan household. Thus, Francis rewrote the Rule as the situation demanded.

Saint Francis wisely submitted his movement to the guidance of the Church. The few Gospel texts that had been the foundation of the early life of the Order gave way to more structure. Ideally, then and now, structure helps all Franciscans contribute to the apostolates of the Church.

The Brotherhood

At the core of the Christian life is Jesus Christ, manifested by the Body of Christ as he exists among his people. The Franciscan Brotherhood is gathered by the Spirit as a body of people called together by God to live a Gospel life of prayer and service. It is a group of people who share a vision of the new life God calls them to, who care for each other in their needs, who form a place where God dwells, a joyous and prayerful people who are sent forth to build the Lord's Kingdom.

A fraternity is a "little flock" of the Lord who live by his Word, who witness to others a way to live the gospel life, who live simply and poor, confidently being sent forth to all their brothers and sisters. A fraternity is a witness that the world is not a world of enemies, but of brothers and sisters of Christ.

A Lay Order

One feature of the Secular Franciscan Order is the role played by obedience. It is a lay order, part of the structure of the Church and loyal to the Church. It therefore has leaders. However, a certain independence of thought and action is characteristic of the Franciscan way of life. Francis himself broke out of the medieval mold. But at the same time, Francis was in touch with the Holy Spirit and recognized the Holy Father as God's voice to him. In the Franciscan movement, there is a balance between independence and authority. It is a movement "for the freedom of the children of God." Obedience is the free and wholehearted cooperation of Secular Franciscans with the decisions of the shepherds of the Church. Free children are not rebellious children. Francis was described soon after his death as a "wholly catholic and apostolic man."

The Fraternity Council

The Secular Franciscan fraternity gathers people together who care for each other, share with each other, pray with each other, support each other. Some are called to be ministers, who serve their brothers and sisters. The fraternity is governed by a council elected by the fraternity to minister to the needs of the brothers and sisters. Each fraternity has a Spiritual Assistant, appointed to help care for the members. The Spiritual Assistant keeps alive the memory of Francis and his unique way of following of Jesus. This person urges, guides and intercedes for the members and unites members and fraternities together. Each fraternity has some members designated as the formation team to introduce new members to the way of Francis.

The duties of the fraternity council, working with the Spiritual Assistant, are: to promote the gospel life, to strengthen the bonds of fraternal love among members and fraternities, to carry on the works of charity and the apostolate; to carry on the general administration of the fraternity.

Within this protecting and strengthening body, the Secular Franciscan strives to live the gospel life and to carry out successfully particular projects of the fraternity. Those called forth by the fraternity to minister to the others should not draw back but know they are blessed by the Lord.

When we come to know Jesus as Francis did, we first need help. We are encouraged to look for it and to grow because of it. But there comes a time, when we need to reach out to help others. We will be thinking more of "how can I help?" rather than "what can I get out of it?" Jesus and Francis gave their lives for the brothers and sisters. We can do no less.

Questions for Reflection—Why must a spiritual movement have structure? What is a fraternity? What is the purpose of the fraternity council? A spiritual assistant?

Connecting With Scripture and Franciscan Writings—David and Saul in 1 Kings, Chapters 25-31; Bodo, *Tales of St. Francis*, pp. 116-117.

Application to Daily Life—Is it possible for any movement to grow in numbers and variety of work without laws and organization? How can we continue to support our brothers and sisters, sharing our faith and strength with them, reaching out to them? Resolve to attend all fraternity gatherings, to commitment yourself to the life and work of the group, and to serve if called upon to do so.

Prayer—Lord, thank you for the friends you have given me along the way of my Christian journey. May we support each other on our way to you. Amen.

From the Rule of the Secular Franciscan Order

20. The Secular Franciscan Order is divided into fraternities of various levels—local, regional, national, and international. Each one has its own moral personality in the Church. These various fraternities are coordinated and united according to the norm of this rule and of the constitutions.

21. On various levels, each fraternity is animated and guided by a council and minister (or president) who are elected by the professed according to the constitutions.

    Their service, which lasts for a definite period, is marked by a ready and willing spirit and is a duty of responsibility to each member and to the community.

    Within themselves the fraternities are structured in different ways according to the various needs of their members and their regions, and under the guidance of their respective council.

22. The local fraternity is to be established canonically. It becomes the basic unit of the whole Order and a visible sign of the Church, the community of love. This should be the privileged place for developing a sense of Church and the

Franciscan vocation and for enlivening the apostolic life of its members.

24. To foster communion among members, the council should organize regular and frequent meetings of the community as well as meeting with other Franciscan groups, especially with youth groups. It should adopt appropriate means for growth in Franciscan and ecclesial life and encourage everyone to a life of fraternity. This communion continues with deceased brothers and sisters through prayer for them.

25. Regarding expenses necessary for the life of the fraternity and the needs of worship, of the apostolate, and of charity, all the brothers and sisters should offer a contribution according to their means. Local fraternities should contribute toward the expense of the higher fraternity councils.

Structure of the Secular Franciscan Order

"In whatever way it seems better to you to please the Lord God and to follow His footprint and poverty, do it with the blessing of the Lord God and my obedience.

—*Saint Francis, "Letter to Brother Leo"*

The fraternity is the basic unit of the Secular Franciscan Order. It is also an independent unit which can stand alone. Yet the need for cooperation between fraternities has led to the formation of various structures so that the kingdom of the Lord may be brought about.

Regions

Fraternities come together as *regions* simply because they are close geographically and find it helpful to work on various projects and to know each other better. Each Region also has a Council to minister to fraternities in the same way as the fraternity has a council to serve its members. The Regional Council makes its own regulations and procedures according to its needs and the needs of those in its care. The general procedures and structure are determined by the National Fraternity.

Regions receive spiritual assistance from the four obediences or jurisdictions, either the Order of Friars Minor (O.F.M.), Order of Friars Minor Capuchin (O.F.M. Cap.), Order of Friars Minor Conventual (O.F.M. Conv.) or Third Order Regular (T.O.R.) or other qualified individuals who are certified by the National Fraternity as spiritual assistants. Formerly, the friar provinces were responsible for the Secular Franciscans and fraternities under their care. Now the National Fraternity of the Secular Franciscan Order and the Regions it represents are independent of the friar provinces. However, Secular Franciscans treasure and respect the spiritual assistance and Franciscan charism which the friars share with them.

International Council

The first meeting of the World Council was held in September, 1975. Secular Franciscans and friars of all four obediences from all over the world met in Rome. Most of the business concerned the working of the World Council, the writing of a new rule and setting up of a world secretariat.

The International Fraternity (CIOFS) is headed by the Minister General and guided by councilors from around the world. A Conference of General Spiritual Assistants provides spiritual assistance to the International Fraternity. Ministers General of the four friar obediences also support the International Fraternity. From the individual fraternity to what is now the International Fraternity through regional and national Federations, the Secular Franciscan Order exhibits a unity of purpose...to live the gospel of the Lord Jesus Christ in witness to the world.

Some Practical Matters

In order to maintain contact with and serve the Secular Franciscans and fraternities, a "visitation" is to be made to the various fraternities. This is a responsibility of the provinces in the Secular Franciscan regions. The purpose of the visitation is to afford an opportunity for the Provincial Assistant to discuss the affairs of the fraternity with the Fraternity assistants and officers; to inquire whether or not the gospel life is being observed, whether the council is functioning properly, whether the fraternity is engaged in works of the apostolate and of charity; if peace and harmony and zeal for gospel living are flourishing. The visitor also looks over the register and other books of the fraternity.

Each fraternity has a common fund to which the members contribute according to their ability and the needs of the Secular Franciscan Order at the various levels. Literature is sent out for acquainting people with the S.F.O.; a fraternity library is customary; instructional material for candidates and professed is necessary. This fund provides supplies for the meetings, stationery, mailing and office supplies, occasional guest speakers, charity to the poor and needy members and others, support for the regional and national operation, apostolic projects of all kinds. No group can function without financial support and so according to your ability and spirit of generosity, you are asked to support the Secular Franciscan Order.

Questions for Reflection—What are the various levels of Secular Franciscan Order structure? What is the purpose of the various levels of fraternities? What is the purpose of a fraternal or pastoral visitation? Of the common fund?

Connecting With Scripture and Franciscan Writings—2 Kings, Chapters 1, 14; Bodo and Susan Saint Sing, *A Retreat with Francis and Clare: Following our Pilgrim Hearts.*

Application to Daily Life—How can the Church advance today with Christians working together? What is my responsibility in the structure of the Secular Franciscan Order to minister to my brothers and sisters? Pray each day for the Secular Franciscan Order, for the leaders in Order, that they may minister to their brothers and sisters well.

Prayer—Praise you, Lord, for people of faith who encircle our planet Earth. Let us become one according to your will. Amen.

From the Rule of the Secular Franciscan Order

26. As a concrete sign of communion and co-responsibility, the councils on various levels, in keeping with the constitutions, shall ask for suitable and well prepared religious for spiritual assistance. They should make this request to the superiors of the four religious Franciscan families, to whom the Secular Fraternity has been united for centuries.

To promote fidelity to the charism as well as observance of the rule and to receive greater support in the life of the fraternity, the minister or president, with the consent of the council, should take care to ask for a regular pastoral visit by the competent religious superiors as well as for a fraternal visit from those of the higher fraternities, according to the norm of the constitutions.

REFLECTION 51

Profession/Commitment

"[N]o one showed me what I had to do, but the Most High Himself revealed to me that I should live according to the pattern of the Holy Gospel."

—*Saint Francis,* The Testament

You have now just about reached the end of a year of careful and prayerful study of the life of a Secular Franciscan. If you are in formation with a Secular Franciscan Fraternity, you may now be invited to make your profession/commitment, that is, a public declaration, officially received by the Church, whereby you promise to strive for holiness by observing the Holy Gospel of our Lord Jesus Christ according to the Rule of the Secular Franciscan Order.

How can this life be described and summarized? Father Benet Fonck, O.F.M., describes it this way:

The Secular Franciscan
is called by God through the Holy Spirit
to observe the Holy Gospel of our Lord Jesus Christ
according to the spirit of Saint Francis
and the heritage of the Franciscan Family
within the world
and in a community of one mind and heart
through a life of prayer (especially the liturgy),
through an ongoing change of heart, and
through Gospel poverty;
and hence is called
to build the spirit of brotherly love among people
by enflaming the world with Gospel values,
by bearing peace and charity,
by instilling justice and dignity,
by being sensitive and loyal to the Church, and
by witnessing to the gospel of Jesus in a public profession.
All of this is done

*through the example and help of Mary, Francis, and the saints
and in imitation of and in intimacy with
Jesus Christ the Lord.*

Profession should take place during the Eucharist, because this special fullness of baptismal life which is sealed and confirmed emphasizes more clearly the task of witnessing to Jesus more effectively in the fraternity, in the Church and throughout the whole world. This ceremony shows forth the fact that now in a new way you give yourself to the Lord Jesus. You are now sent forth in a new way by the Spirit for the work of the Lord. By profession you enter into a new relationship with the other members of your fraternity.

Fraternity

In committing yourself to walk in the way of Jesus, you also commit yourself to your brothers and sisters. God does not call you for yourself alone but as brothers and sisters. We belong to a community, a fraternity. We learn about Jesus from the community of faith. We see Francis' way with the aid of his followers. Committing oneself to the Lord to observe the gospel cannot be done alone. We need the help and support and prayers of our brothers and sisters. While the fraternity does not meet too often, the members are called to care for each other, pray with each other, share with each other, work with each other, because Jesus lives among us.

Questions for Reflection—Is the Franciscan way of life one you choose to follow all the days of your life? How will a fraternity help you to remain faithful to following Francis and Jesus?

Connecting With Scripture and Franciscan Writings—The revolt against David and his death in 2 Kings, Chapters 15-24. Continue reading the Old Testament. Continue Bodo and Saint Sing, *A Retreat with Francis and Clare.*

Application to Daily Life—Reflect on where you have been in your life, how the Lord has been working. Admit your weaknesses and failures and trust in the power of the Lord to change you. Fear nothing and nobody. Prepare yourself in prayer for making your profession. Try to understand what you are doing in being professed. Give yourself to Jesus. Promise to work for him and his kingdom.

Prayer—What way am I to go from this point in my life, Lord, now that I know your faithful Francis better? How am I to follow his way, your way? Show me, Lord. Lead me, Lord. I am yours. Amen.

From the Rule of the Secular Franciscan Order

23. Requests for admission to the Secular Franciscan Order must be presented to the local fraternity, whose council decides upon the acceptance of new brothers and sisters.

    Admission into the Order is gradually attained through a time of initiation, a period of formation of at least one year, and profession of the rule. The entire community is engaged in this process of growth by its own manner of living. The age for profession and the distinctive Franciscan sign are regulated by the statutes.

    Profession by its nature is a permanent commitment.

    Members who find themselves in particular difficulties should discuss their problems with the council in fraternal dialogue. Withdrawal or permanent dismissal from the Order, if necessary, is an act of the fraternity council according to the norm of the constitutions.

Let Us Begin Again, and Again, and Again....

"I have done what was mine to do; may the Lord teach you yours."
—*Saint Francis*

Once professed in the Secular Franciscan Order, you have completed a task and entered a new world, only to begin again. Profession is a door through which you enter a new life—a life of the gospel, a life of the beatitudes. You will begin to walk with the Lord in his life and in his way and in his truth. You can expect to be discouraged or frustrated or as the Bible says "in the desert" at times, but believe more and more strongly that Jesus is walking with you. He says, "Do not be afraid." As you respond to his call and as you walk with him, you will find yourself serving your brothers and sisters. You will reach out to them.

Knowing the Lord

Perhaps we should call attention to something you have read in Father Murray Bodo's book, *Francis: The Journey and the Dream*. He describes well how Francis came to know Jesus, *and knew himself for the first time.* Francis knew himself as the *Poverello,* "the little poor man," whose strength was in the Lord. He experienced the Lord working in his life. We need to do the same.

Know that the Lord is working in your life and in your fraternity. Jesus says: "I will be with you." Difficulties, resentments, striving for power and jealousies will crop up in your life and in the lives of your brothers and sisters. But Jesus doesn't abandon us; he stays with us, patiently comforting, guiding, teaching, but also convicting us of sin and weakness. Jesus has a sense of urgency in the Gospel: "There is no time to lose. The life we live and the work we do is important for each of us and for his kingdom."

Prayer and Ministry

Strive to develop a deep life of prayer. Continue to set aside a period of time each day for prayer, both in praise of God and in intercession for your brothers and sisters. All of us are in need of the mercy of God.

Strive also to minister to your brothers and sisters, both in the fraternity, in your families and among your friends. The Lord calls us to be peacemakers, calling us to prayer to repair all the destruction which violence causes in the world. Reach out beyond yourself as Francis did. Reach out as Jesus did.

And finally, read the Word of the Lord every day, reflect on it, let it "make a home in you." Make your daily decisions on the basis of what Jesus said and did. Believe that the Spirit continually calls us together to form the Body of Jesus today.

Invite Others to Join You

There is a little "in" joke about the Secular Franciscan Order that says, "The S.F.O. is the best kept secret in the Church." But we are not to keep good things for ourselves. Share with others about what the Lord is doing for you. It is only natural to tell others about this new way of life you have accepted and invite them to join you. What the Lord is doing for you, he can do for them.

Questions for Reflection—What does profession mean? Why do you make your commitment within a group of people who are called as you are, a fraternity? To what work is Jesus calling you?

Connecting With Scripture and Franciscan Writings—Continue to read the sacred Scriptures; select new Franciscan readings from the Resource List at the back of this book.

Application to Daily Life—Try to look at all those around you as "brothers and sisters" whom you love and cherish. Observe how this affects your view of the world.

Prayer—Loving God, I give you honor, thanks and praise. You forgive me when I fail to live according to the Gospel. You encourage me when I do follow your way. I ask for the faith and courage to begin again and again to follow Jesus, my Lord and Savior. Amen.

Resources

May the Lord give you a new hope every morning and joy to accompany you through the day.

Resources

An extensive Franciscan Resource List is available from:

Secular Franciscan Resource List (Kirksville, Mo.: National Formation Commission of The National Fraternity of the Secular Franciscan Order—U.S.A., 1997) (1-888-UMBRIA2).

Books

Anthony, Edd, O.F.M., *Canticle of Brother Sun* (Cincinnati: St. Anthony Messenger Press and Franciscan Communications, 1989).

Armstrong, Regis J., O.F.M. Cap., and Ignatius Brady, O.F.M., *Francis and Clare: The Complete Works, Classics of Western Spirituality* (New York: Paulist Press, 1982).

___, *Catch Me a Rainbow: The Franciscan Journey* (Lindborg, Kan.: Barbo-Carlson Enterprises, 1990).

Bach, Lester, O.F.M. Cap., *Catch Me a Rainbow, Too* (Lindborg, Kan.: Barbo-Carlson Enterprises, 1998).

Baker, Teresa, S.F.O., *Gospel Living Every Day of Our Lives: A Formation Guide to the Rule of the Secular Franciscan Order* (Lindborg, Kan.: Barbo-Carlson Enterprises, 1998).

Bodo, Murray, O.F.M., *Francis: The Journey and the Dream* (Cincinnati: St. Anthony Messenger Press, rev. ed., 1988).

___, *Francisco: El Viaje y el Sueno* (Spanish language edition) (Cincinnati: St. Anthony Messenger Press, 1994).

___, *Clare: A Light in the Garden* (Cincinnati: St. Anthony Messenger Press, rev. ed., 1992).

___, *Tales of St. Francis: Ancient Stories for Contemporary Living* (Cincinnati: St. Anthony Messenger Press, 1992).

____, *Through the Year with Francis of Assisi: Daily Meditations from His Words and Life* (Cincinnati: St. Anthony Messenger Press, 1993).

____, *The Way of St. Francis: The Challenge of Franciscan Spirituality for Everyone* (Cincinnati: St. Anthony Messenger Press, 1995).

____ and Susan Saint Sing, *A Retreat With Francis and Clare of Assisi: Following Our Pilgrim Hearts* (Cincinnati: St. Anthony Messenger Press, 1996).

Brady, Ignatius, O.F.M., *The Prayers of Saint Francis.* (Ann Arbor, Mich.: Servant Books, 1987).

Carney, Margaret, *The First Franciscan Woman: Clare of Assisi & Her Form of Life* (Quincy, Ill.: Franciscan Press, 1993).

Chesterton, G. K., St. Francis of Assisi (New York: George H. Doran Co., 1924).

Cook, William R., *Francis of Assisi: The Way of Poverty and Humility* (Wilmington, Del.: Michael Glazier, 1989).

Dennis, Marie; Joseph Nangle, O.F.M.; Cynthia Moe-Lobeda; and Stuart Taylor, *St. Francis and the Foolishness of God* (Maryknoll, N.Y.: Orbis Books, 1993).

Fonck, Benet, O.F.M., *To Cling with All Her Heart to Him: The Spirituality of St. Clare of Assisi* (Quincy, Ill.: Franciscan Press, 1996).

Fortini, Arnaldo, *Francis of Assisi* (New York: Seabury, 1980).

Haase, Albert, *Swimming in the Sun: Discovering the Lord's Prayer with Francis of Assisi and Thomas Merton* (Cincinnati: St. Anthony Messenger Press, 1993).

Habig, Marion A., O.F.M., ed., Secular Franciscan Companion (Chicago: Franciscan Herald Press, rev. ed., 1987).

Hutchinson, Gloria, *Six Ways to Pray from Six Great Saints* (Cincinnati: St. Anthony Messenger Press, 1982).

____, *Clare of Assisi: The Anchored Souls* (Cincinnati: St. Anthony Messenger Press, 1982).

Jobe, Sara Lee, *Footsteps in Assisi* (New York: Paulist Press, 1996).

Kirvan, John, *Peace of Heart: Based on the Life and Teachings of Francis of Assisi* (Notre Dame, Ind.: Ave Maria Press, 1995).

Leclerc, Eloi, *Wisdom of the Poverello* (Chicago: Franciscan Herald Press, 1989).

Moorman, John R. H., *Richest of Poor Men: The Spirituality of St. Francis of Assisi* (Huntington, Ind.: Our Sunday Visitor, 1977).

Miller, Ramona, and Ingrid Peterson, *Praying with Clare of Assisi* (Winona, Minn.: St. Mary's Press, 1994).

Noonan, Hugh, O.F.M., and Roy Gasnick, O.F.M., *Francis of Assisi: The Song Goes On* (Cincinnati: St. Anthony Messenger Press, 1994).

Normile, Patti, S.F.O., *Following Francis of Assisi: A Spirituality for Daily Living* (Cincinnati: St. Anthony Messenger Press, 1996).

Pazzelli, Raffael, *St. Francis and the Third Order* (Chicago: Franciscan Herald Press, 1989)

Portasik, Richard, O.F.M., *Way of Life*, available from Franciscan Friars, 232 S. Home Ave., Pittsburgh, Penn. 15202.

Saint Sing, Susan, *St. Francis, Poet of Creation: The Story of the Canticle of Brother Sun* (Chicago: Franciscan Herald Press, 1985).

S.F.O.: Catch Our Spirit (Cincinnati: St. Anthony Messenger Press/ Franciscan Communications, 1987).

Wintz, Jack, O.F.M., *Lights: Revelations of God's Goodness.* (Cincinnati: St. Anthony Messenger Press, 1995).

Video

Brother Sun, Sister Moon. Hollywood, Cal.: Paramount Pictures, 1973. (Order from Vision Videos.)

Hodgson, Karen, *Clare of Assisi.* Oblate Media. Distributed by St. Anthony Messenger Press, Cincinnati.

The Message of St. Francis for Today. With Michael Crosby, O.F.M. Distributed by St. Anthony Messenger Press, Cincinnati.

Poor Clares: A Hidden Presence. Assisi, Italy: Oriente Occidente Productions. Distributed by The Franciscan Store or St. Anthony Messenger Press, 1994.

Sbicca, Arturo, *St. Francis of Assisi.* Distributed by St. Anthony Messenger Press, Cincinnati., 1992.

___, *St. Clare of Assisi.* Oriente Occidente Productions. Distributed by St. Anthony Messenger Press, Cincinnati.

___, *St. Francis of Assisi.* Oriente Occidente Productions. Distributed by St. Anthony Messenger Press, Cincinnati.

Thomson, Christa Marie, O.S.F., *Discovering our Myth: Our Challenge for Today*. Lindborg, Kan.: Barbo-Carlson Enterprises.

Wintz, Jack, O.F.M., *Franciscan Holy Ground: Where Francis and Clare Found God*. St. Anthony Messenger Press, Cincinnati, 1997.

Audio

Bodo, Murray, O.F.M., *A Mosaic of Francis: Making His Way Our Own* (Cincinnati: St. Anthony Messenger Press, 1986).

___, *Francis: The Journey and the Dream* (Cincinnati: St. Anthony Messenger Press, 1986).

___, and Susan Saint Sing, *The Song of St. Francis: A Celebration of the Seasons of His Life* (Cincinnati: St. Anthony Messenger Press, 1980).

Harkins, Conrad, O.F.M., *Francis of Assisi: Enduring Values*. (Cincinnati: St. Anthony Messenger Press, 1995).

Rohr, Richard, O.F.M., *Letting Go: A Spirituality of Subtraction* (Cincinnati: St. Anthony Messenger Press, 1987).

___, *Embracing Christ as Francis Did: In the Church of the Poor* (Cincinnati: St. Anthony Messenger Press, 1984).

Internet

Useful for exploring Franciscanism in general and the Secular Franciscan Order in particular:

http://listserv.american.edu/catholic/franciscan
A major resource on the Internet for all things Franciscan.

http://ofs.communitech.net/SFO.HTM

http://listserv.american.edu/catholic/franciscan/cord/cord.html
Articles reprinted from *The Cord: A Franciscan Spiritual Review* published by Franciscan Institute at St. Bonaventure University.

http://www.americancatholic.org
Home page of St. Anthony Messenger Press

Franciscan Resource Centers

TAU-USA (newsletter of the national fraternity)
c/o Dolores Smelko, S.F.O.
RD 1, Box 155,
Anita, Penn. 15711
E-mail: deesmelko@penn.com

Barbo-Carlson Enterprises
P.O. Box 189
Lindsborg, Kan. 67456-0189
Phone: 785-227-2364
Fax: 785-227-3360

Franciscan Resources
P.O. Box 350
Menahga, Minn. 56464
Phone Orders: 1-800-772-6910
Fax: 1-218-837-5447
E-mail: franres@wcta.net

St. Anthony Messenger Press
1615 Republic Street
Cincinnati, Ohio 45210
Phone: 513-241-5615
Toll free: 800-488-0488
E-mail: StAnthony@AmericanCatholic.org

Institute for Contemporary Franciscan Life
(correspondence program in Franciscan studies)
St. Francis College
Phone: 814-472-3219
E-mail: ICFL@SFCPA.EDU

The Franciscan Store
165 E. Pulaski Street
Pulaski, Wis. 54162
Phone: 920-822-5833
Fax: 920-822-5423

The Rule of the
Secular Franciscan Order

*"May whoever observes all this be filled
in heaven with the blessing of the
most high Father, and on earth
with that of his beloved Son,
together with the Holy Spirit,
the Comforter."*

*—Blessing of Saint Francis
from* The Testament

The Rule of the Secular Franciscan Order

—Approved by Pope Paul VI, June 24, 1978

PROLOGUE: Exhortation of Saint Francis to the Brothers and Sisters
           in Penance

In the name of the Lord!

Concerning Those Who Do Penance

All who love the Lord with their whole heart, with their whole soul and mind, with all their strength (cf. Mark 12:30), and love their neighbors as themselves (cf. Matthew 22:39) and hate their bodies with their vices and sins, and receive the Body and Blood of our Lord Jesus Christ, and produce worthy fruits of penance;

Oh, how happy and blessed are these men and women because "the spirit of the Lord will rest upon them" (cf. Isaiah 11:2) and he will make "his home and dwelling among them" (cf. John 14:23), and they are the sons of the heavenly Father (cf. Matthew 5:45), whose works they do, and they are the spouses, brothers, and mothers of our Lord Jesus Christ (cf. Matthew 12:50).

We are spouses, when by the Holy Spirit the faithful soul is united with our Lord Jesus Christ, we are brothers to him when we fulfill "the will of the Father who is in heaven" (Matthew 12:50).

We are mothers, when we carry him in our heart and body (cf. 1 Corinthians 6:20) through divine love and a pure and sincere conscience; we give birth to him through a holy life which must give light to others by example (cf. Matthew 5:16).

Oh, how glorious it is to have a great and holy Father in Heaven! Oh how glorious it is to have such a beautiful and admirable Spouse, the Holy Paraclete!

Oh, how glorious it is to have such a Brother and such a Son, loved, beloved, humble, peaceful, sweet, lovable, and desirable above all: Our Lord Jesus Christ, who gave up his life for his sheep (cf. John 10:15) and prayed to the Father saying:

"O Holy Father, protect them with your name (cf. John 17:11) whom you gave me out of the world. I entrusted to them the message you entrusted to me and they received it. They have known that in truth I came from You, they have believed that it was You who sent me. For these I pray, not for the word (cf. John 17:9). Bless and consecrate them, and I consecrate myself for their sakes. I do not pray for them alone; I pray also for those who will believe in me through their word (cf. John 17:20) that they may be holy by being one as we are (cf. John 17:11). And I desire, Father, to have them in my company where I am to see this glory of mine in your kingdom" (cf. John 17:6-24).

Concerning Those Who Do Not Do Penance

But all those men and women who are not doing penance and do not receive the Body and Blood of our Lord Jesus Christ and live in vices and sin and yield to evil concupiscence and to the wicked desires of the flesh, and do not observe what they have promised to the Lord, and are slaves to the world in their bodies, by carnal desires and the anxieties and cares of this life (cf. John 8:41);

These are blind, because they do not see the true light, our Lord Jesus Christ; they do not have spiritual wisdom because they do not have the Son of God who is the true wisdom of the Father. Concerning them, it is said "Their skill was swallowed up" (Psalms 107:27) and "cursed are those who turn away from your commands" (Psalms 119:21). They see and acknowledge, they know and do bad things and knowingly destroy their own souls.

See, you who are blind, deceived by your enemies, the world, the flesh and the devil, for it is pleasant to the body to commit sin and it is bitter to make it serve God because all vices and sins come out and "proceed from the heart of man" as the Lord says in the gospel (cf. Matthew 7:21). And you have nothing in this world and in the next, and you thought you would possess the vanities of this world for a long time.

But you have been deceived, for the day and the hour will come to which you give no thought and which you do not know and of which you are ignorant. The body grows infirm, death approaches, and so it dies a bitter death, and no matter where or when or how man dies, in the guilt of sin, without penance or satisfaction, through he can make satisfaction but does not do it.

The devil snatches the soul from his body with such anguish and tribulation that no one can know it except he who endures it, and all the talents and power and "knowledge and wisdom" (2 Chronicles 1:17) which they thought they had will be taken away from them (cf. Luke 8:18; Mark 4:25), and they leave their goods to relatives and friends who take and divide them and say afterwards "Cursed be his soul because he could have given us more, he could have acquired more than he did." The worms eat up the body and so they have lost body and soul during this short earthly life and will go into the inferno where they will suffer torture without end.

All those into whose hands this letter shall have come we ask in the charity that is God (cf. 1 John 4:17) to accept kindly and with divine love the fragrant words of our Lord Jesus Christ quoted above. And let those who do not know how to read have them read to them.

And may they keep them in their mind and carry them out, in a holy manner to the end, because they are "spirit and life" (John 6:64).

And those who will not do this will have to render "an account on the day of judgment" (cf. Matthew 12:36) before the tribunal of our Lord Jesus Christ (cf. Romans 14:10).

Chapter One: The Secular Franciscan Order (S.F.O.)

1. The Franciscan family, as one among many spiritual families raised up by the Holy Spirit in the Church, unites all members of the People of God—laity, religious, and priests—who recognize that they are called to follow Christ in the footsteps of Saint Francis of Assisi.

   In various ways and forms but in life-giving union with each other, they intend to make present the charism of their common Seraphic Father in the life and mission of the Church.

2. The Secular Franciscan Order holds a special place in this family circle. It is an organic union of all Catholic fraternities scattered throughout the world and open to every group of the faithful. In these fraternities the brothers and sisters, led by the Spirit, strive for perfect charity in their own secular state. By their profession they pledge themselves to live the gospel in the manner of Saint Francis by means of this rule approved by the Church.

3. The present rule, succeeding "Memoriale Propositi" (1221) and the rules approved by the Supreme Pontiffs Nicholas IV and Leo XIII, adapts the Secular Franciscan Order to the needs and expectations of the Holy Church in the conditions of changing times. Its interpretation belongs to the Holy See and its application will be made by the General Constitutions and particular statutes.

Chapter Two: The Way of Life

4. The rule and life of the Secular Franciscans is this: to observe the gospel of our Lord Jesus Christ by following the example of Saint

Francis of Assisi, who made Christ the inspiration and the center of his life with God and people.

Christ, the gift of the Father's love, is the way to him, the truth into which the Holy Spirit leads us, and the life which he has come to give abundantly.

Secular Franciscans should devote themselves especially to careful reading of the gospel, going from gospel to life and life to the gospel.

5. Secular Franciscans, therefore, should seek to encounter the living and active person of Christ in their brothers and sisters, in Sacred Scripture, in the Church, and in liturgical activity. The faith of Saint Francis, who often said "I see nothing bodily of the Most High Son of God in this world except his most holy body and blood," should be the inspiration and pattern of their eucharistic life.

6. They have been made living members of the Church by being buried and raised with Christ in baptism; they have been united more intimately with the Church by profession. Therefore, they should go forth as witnesses and instruments of her mission among all people, proclaiming Christ by their life and words.

    Called like Saint Francis to rebuild the Church and inspired by his example, let them devote themselves energetically to living in full communion with the pope, bishops, and priests, fostering an open and trusting dialogue of apostolic effectiveness and creativity.

7. United by their vocation as "brothers and sisters of penance," and motivated by the dynamic power of the gospel, let them conform their thoughts and deeds to those of Christ by means of that radical interior change which the Gospel itself calls "conversion." Human frailty makes it necessary that this conversion be carried out daily."

    On this road to renewal the sacrament of reconciliation is the privileged sign of the Father's mercy and the source of grace.

8. As Jesus was the true worshiper of the Father, so let prayer and contemplation be the soul of all they are and do.

    Let them participate in the sacramental life of the Church, above all the Eucharist. Let them join in liturgical prayer in one of the forms proposed by the Church, reliving the mysteries of the life of Christ.

9. The Virgin Mary, humble servant of the Lord, was open to his every word and call. She was embraced by Francis with indescribable love and declared the protectress and advocate of his family. The Secular Franciscans should express their ardent love for her by imi-

tating her complete self-giving and by praying earnestly and confidently.

10. Uniting themselves to the redemptive obedience of Jesus, who placed his will into the Father's hands, let them faithfully fulfill the duties proper to their various circumstances of life. Let them also follow the poor and crucified Christ, witnessing to him even in difficulties and persecutions.

11. Trusting in the Father, Christ chose for himself and his mother a poor and humble life, even though he valued created things attentively and lovingly. Let the Secular Franciscans seek a proper spirit of detachment from temporal goods by simplifying their own material needs. Let them be mindful that according to the gospel they are stewards of the goods received for the benefit of God's children.

Thus, in the spirit of "the Beatitudes," and as pilgrims and strangers on their way to the home of the Father, they should strive to purify their hearts from every tendency and yearning for possession and power.

12. Witnessing to the good yet to come and obliged to acquire purity of heart because of the vocation they have embraced, they should set themselves free to love God and their brothers and sisters.

13. As the Father sees in every person the features of his Son, the first born of many brothers and sisters, so the Secular Franciscans with a gentle and courteous spirit accept all people as a gift of the Lord and an image of Christ.

A sense of community will make them joyful and ready to place themselves on an equal basis with all people, especially with the lowly for whom they shall strive to create conditions of life worthy of people redeemed by Christ.

14. Secular Franciscans, together with all people of good will, are called to build a more fraternal and evangelical world so that the kingdom of God may be brought about more effectively. Mindful that anyone "who follows Christ, the perfect man, becomes more of a man himself," let them exercise their responsibilities competently in the Christian spirit of service.

15. Let them individually and collectively be in the forefront in promoting justice by the testimony of their human lives and their courageous initiatives. Especially in the field of public life, they should make definite choices in harmony with their faith.

16. Let them esteem work both as a gift and as a sharing in the creation, redemption, and service of the human community.

17. In their family they should cultivate the Franciscan spirit of peace, fidelity, and respect for life, striving to make it a sign of a world already renewed in Christ.

By living the grace of matrimony, husbands and wives in particular should bear witness in the world to the love of Christ for his Church. They should joyfully accompany their children on their human and spiritual journey by providing a simple and open Christian education and being attentive to the vocation of each child.

18. Moreover they should respect all creatures, animate and inanimate, which "bear the imprint of the Most High," and they should strive to move from the temptation of exploiting creation to the Franciscan concept of universal kinship.

19. Mindful that they are bearers of peace which must be built up unceasingly, they should seek out ways of unity and fraternal harmony through dialogue, trusting in the presence of the divine seed in everyone and in the transforming power of love and pardon.

Messengers of perfect joy in every circumstance, they should strive to bring joy and hope to others.

Since they are immersed in the resurrection of Christ, which gives true meaning to Sister Death, let them serenely tend toward the ultimate encounter with the Father.

Chapter Three: Life in Fraternity

20. The Secular Franciscan Order is divided into fraternities of various levels—local, regional, national, and international. Each one has its own moral personality in the Church. These various fraternities are coordinated and united according to the norm of this rule and of the constitutions.

21. On various levels, each fraternity is animated and guided by a council and minister (or president) who are elected by the professed according to the constitutions.

Their service, which lasts for a definite period, is marked by a ready and willing spirit and is a duty of responsibility to each member and to the community.

Within themselves the fraternities are structured in different ways according to the various needs of their members and their regions, and under the guidance of their respective council.

22. The local fraternity is to be established canonically. It becomes the basic unit of the whole Order and a visible sign of the Church, the

community of love. This should be the privileged place for developing a sense of Church and the Franciscan vocation and for enlivening the apostolic life of its members.

23. Requests for admission to the Secular Franciscan Order must be presented to the local fraternity, whose council decides upon the acceptance of new brothers and sisters.

   Admission into the Order is gradually attained through a time of initiation, a period of formation of at least one year, and profession of the rule. The entire community is engaged in this process of growth by its own manner of living. The age for profession and the distinctive Franciscan sign are regulated by the statutes.

   Profession by its nature is a permanent commitment.

   Members who find themselves in particular difficulties should discuss their problems with the council in fraternal dialogue. Withdrawal or permanent dismissal from the Order, if necessary, is an act of the fraternity council according to the norm of the constitutions.

24. To foster communion among members, the council should organize regular and frequent meetings of the community as well as meeting with other Franciscan groups, especially with youth groups. It should adopt appropriate means for growth in Franciscan and ecclesial life and encourage everyone to a life of fraternity. This communion continues with deceased brothers and sisters through prayer for them.

25. Regarding expenses necessary for the life of the fraternity and the needs of worship, of the apostolate, and of charity, all the brothers and sisters should offer a contribution according to their means. Local fraternities should contribute toward the expense of the higher fraternity councils.

26. As a concrete sign of communion and coresponsibility, the councils on various levels, in keeping with the constitutions, shall ask for suitable and well prepared religious for spiritual assistance. They should make this request to the superiors of the four religious Franciscan families, to whom the Secular Fraternity has been united for centuries.

To promote fidelity to the charism as well as observance of the rule and to receive greater support in the life of the fraternity, the minister or president, with the consent of the council, should take care to ask for a regular pastoral visit by the competent religious superiors as well as for a fraternal visit from those of the higher fraternities, according to the norm of the constitutions.

Invitation

*M*ay the Lord Give You Peace

Francis of Assisi, who was called the little poor man, rediscovered the Gospel as a way of life. Thousands and millions in his three Orders of people have followed Francis in his rediscovery of the Gospel. The new Rule of the Secular Franciscans put it this way: The rule and life of the Secular Franciscans is this: to observe the gospel of our Lord Jesus Christ by following the example of Saint Francis of Assisi, who made Christ the inspiration and center of his life with God and people (No. 4).

The Secular Franciscan Order, formerly called the Third Order of Saint Francis, is a community of men and women in the world who seek to pattern their lives after Saint Francis of Assisi, and through him, Christ Jesus.

It has been in existence for over 750 years. Today, it includes over 700,000 members throughout the world, 40,000 in the United States alone. We invite you to join us. We believe that we have been called by the Spirit of God to live the Gospel, a vocation we cannot fulfill alone; we know we need other Christians, a community or fraternity which helps us in praying and serving others.

As Saint Francis experienced a conversion of his life, so he leads us into a new world through a conversion experience. Each member is led through various steps of (1) looking it over, (2) trying it out through a program of prayer, study and action, and (3) making a profession of the Secular Franciscan Rule as their own way of life.

We are not called to leave the world, but to transform it. We remain in our families, maintain and deepen our friendships. But as we live our lives, our ideas, our prayer and our life-style grow and change. The Spirit gives us light and power to transform and free us from all that hinders us from loving God and each other.

We are brothers and sisters in a fraternity, expecting prayer and support from each other.

We read and pray and live the Gospel to learn the ways of Christ.

We are joined with Jesus and each other in the Eucharist.

We are able to deepen our life of prayer and our union with God.

We have special concern for the works of peace and reconciliation.

We seek to live simply, value persons above possessions, sharing what we have with others.

We strengthen our loyalty to the Church and her shepherds, as to the Lord.

We strive to help the sick, the poor and the oppressed.

We are able to develop leadership skills, receiving the gifts of the Lord with gratitude.

We receive strength to overcome the difficulties of life.

We receive healing from the Lord and each other.

Our Rule of Life has been revised and approved by our Holy Father, Pope Paul VI. The Secular Franciscans have the same vision and mission as the Church herself.

We invite you to join us. Just inquire at the address or phone number in the Resources section. But whether you join us or not, we pray that the Lord give you peace!